GOVERNANCE HANDBOOK
for Friends Schools

Second Edition

Prepared by
Irene McHenry, Ph.D. and Ginny Christensen, Ed.D.

from the original work by
Irene McHenry, Friends Council on Education and
Tom Hoopes, Philadelphia Yearly Meeting (2002)

Friends Council on Education

1507 Cherry Street, Philadelphia, PA 19102
www.friendscouncil.org

ABOUT FRIENDS SCHOOLS

Friends schools have a wide sphere of influence. They preserve an experimental attitude and are fearless in holding to standards of scholarship, to equality of opportunity regardless of race and nationality, to simplicity of environment, to democracy in administration, and positive religious teaching.

We are all educators: we all create attitudes and influence opinion, help or hinder spiritual nurture. We must keep clear, amidst many activities, our central purpose. Beyond the beautiful and creative arts, the useful and practical subjects, the concern with science and culture, the soul awaits God's quickening breath. Without it humankind dies.

Esther L. Duke, Rachel Cadbury, and Anna Brinton, 1941, in *Handbook for Committee Members of Friends Schools*, Philadelphia Yearly Meeting, 1958 (first edition).

Governance Handbook for Friends Schools
ISBN: 978-0-9824030-1-3
© 2010 by the Friends Council on Education
Irene McHenry, Ph.D., and Ginny Christensen, Ed.D.

All rights reserved.

Table of Contents

Acknowledgements vii

Introduction ix
- *Why is this handbook necessary and timely?*
- *How can best use be made of this handbook?*

CHAPTER 1

Friends School Governance: An Overview 1
- *What is unique about a Friends school?*
- *What distinguishes governance authority in a Friends school from that of other schools?*
- *What is the role of Quaker practice in Friends school governance?*
- *What does it mean for a school to be in a "care relationship" with a Friends Meeting?*

CHAPTER 2

Mission and Fiduciary Strength 5
- *How is its mission especially significant for the board of a Friends school?*
- *What are the fiduciary responsibilities of the board as they relate to the mission?*
- *How involved should the board be in financial management?*
- *What are the board's and head's roles in fiduciary planning?*
- *How and when should the board address budgeting and financial issues?*
- *What special considerations should a Friends school board make in setting tuition, financial aid, and salary budgets?*
- *What other mission imperatives might be specific to Friends schools?*
- *What is the board's responsibility for school accreditation?*

CHAPTER 3

Decision Making 13

- *What is the Quaker decision-making process?*
- *How does the Friends decision-making process work in a Quaker meeting for business?*
- *What distinguishes decision making in a Friends school from that in a Friends Meeting?*
- *What are the benefits of Quaker-based decision making in a Friends school?*
- *How can we use the Quaker-based decision-making process in a Friends school?*
- *What is the role of a leader in using the Quaker-based decision-making process in a Friends school?*
- *Who makes decisions in a Friends school?*
- *What decisions are the responsibility of the board in a Friends school?*

CHAPTER 4

Roles and Responsibilities 23

- *How can we develop a clear understanding of roles, responsibilities, and inclusivity, especially as these relate to decision making in a Friends school?*
- *Does the board focus on policy and the head on operations?*
- *Who has the ultimate leadership role — the head or the board?*
- *How can the board ensure that it is staying within its role?*

CHAPTER 5

Shared Vision and Strategic Planning 31

- *What is the significance of a shared vision in a Friends school?*
- *How does the shared vision inform the strategic plan for a Friends school?*
- *How does a Friends school board engage in strategic planning?*

CHAPTER 6

Advancement 37

- *What is the work of the board in building a strong foundation for fundraising and marketing in a Friends school?*

- *How are individual board members in a Friends school involved in the work of fundraising?*
- *How does the fundraising culture and practice of the school strengthen the school's identity as a Friends school?*
- *What are some common challenges for Friends school board members' work in fundraising?*
- *How are board members in a Friends school involved in the work of marketing?*

CHAPTER 7

Effective Board Process 43

- *What does effective board/committee process look like in Friends school governance?*
- *How do openness, confidentiality, and trust factor into the work of a Friends school board?*
- *What are best practice methods used by board clerks for leading effective meetings?*
- *What are the general responsibilities of the committees of the board and what responsibilities do specific committees have?*
- *Can board committees include individuals who are not trustees?*
- *How do we obtain the best members for highly engaged and effective committee and board functioning?*
- *How does a Friends school board prepare for thoughtful and timely leadership succession?*
- *How can a board best orient new members?*
- *What can improve the flow of work from the board out to committees, and from committees back to the board?*
- *How can we move our board meetings toward a dynamic dialogue about substantive issues?*

CHAPTER 8

Creating an Optimum Culture for School Leadership and Governance 57

- *How can we create an optimum culture for school leadership and governance?*
- *How can we tell if the board is strong?*
- *What is known about conflict at the governance level in school life?*
- *What processes do Friends schools use to work with conflict in school life?*

- *How does the board know how the head is doing?*
- *What are respectful and supportive methods for learning about the head's performance and working on issues that may arise?*
- *What is an "executive session" of the board and when is it appropriate to hold an executive session?*
- *What if members of the community voice critical complaints about the head directly to members of the board?*
- *What attitudes and tools are helpful in the heat of discussion?*

CHAPTER 9

Relationships Across the School Community 71

- *Why is it important for the board to nurture good relationships in a Friends school?*
- *How can board members, individually and collectively, nurture good relationships with each of the constituencies in the school community?*
- *Given the crucial importance of supporting and nurturing the head of school, are there specific things that the board is encouraged to do in this regard?*
- *Given the special importance of the partnership between the clerk of the board and the head of school, what can be done to support and nurture this relationship?*

References 79

Glossary 81

Appendix A — Resources for Further Study 87

Appendix B — Friends Education Position Statements 89

Acknowledgements

We are grateful for the insight and wisdom from the 1986 *Handbook for Committee Members of Friends Schools* as well as the authors and contributors to the first edition (2001) of the *Governance Handbook for Friends Schools*. In dynamic relationship with external changes, the internal operations of Friends schools continue to evolve and new Friends schools continue to sprout from the commitment and vision of Friends and Friends school alumni/ae across the country. Given the important role that Friends schools play in the educational landscape across the country, we have updated this proactive set of guidelines to support the continued good stewardship of Friends schools.

We express appreciation to the thousands of trustees whose past and current board service to Friends schools has contributed to the development of sound practices. We are grateful to the Monthly, Quarterly, and Yearly Friends Meetings that provide thoughtful leadership and care for Friends governance. We also express appreciation for the fine work embodied in the *Trustee Handbook* of the National Association of Independent Schools, which has proven itself to be a valued resource for all involved with school governance. It is our sincere hope that this *Governance Handbook for Friends Schools* and its companion *Principles of Good Practice for Friends School Boards* find valuable use by trustees and heads of all Friends schools.

We give special thanks to Harry Hammond, Heather Hoerle, Jennifer Karsten, Arthur Larrabee and Nancy van Arkel for their generous contributions to the writing of this *Governance Handbook*. We appreciate the editorial work of Barbara Kraus-Blackney, Dorothy Flanagan, Ruth Greenberger, and the time and expertise of our extraordinary production editor, Sarah Sweeney-Denham.

Introduction

The purpose of the *Governance Handbook for Friends Schools* is to serve as a useful resource for boards and trustees of Friends schools, the heads of these institutions, and the Friends Meetings that are in care relationships with Friends schools. We believe that this volume will provide a valuable governance perspective and resources to boards of private and independent schools, in addition to supporting those entrusted with the guidance of Friends schools, in their work towards effective institutional governance and fidelity to the traditions of Quaker education.

Throughout this volume we refer to the governing body of a school as the "board" in order to maintain consistency with the language of the larger world of independent school governance, and for the sake of clarity. For those Friends schools that are under the fiduciary oversight of a Friends Meeting, and of which the governing body is therefore a committee of the Meeting, "board" may be read as "school committee" without loss of meaning.

Why is this handbook necessary and timely?

While Friends schools continue to be guided by the over-arching vision and spiritual values of the Religious Society of Friends, it is important for us to recognize that Friends schools are also operating as "independent schools," i.e., private educational organizations with particular missions, which operate with a non-profit business structure and must compete in the marketplace with other private schools, as well as with public schools, charter schools, and home schooling options. As such, good governance requires that we continue to honor the historical priorities of Quaker education, while simultaneously living up to our responsibility as stewards of independent schools.

The rationale for this *Governance Handbook for Friends Schools*, then, is to bridge the gap between the Friends school and independent school perspectives and to provide a helpful resource in this process. Accordingly, this document has been written to be used in concert with the *Trustee Handbook* of the National Association of Independent Schools (NAIS) to support Friends school governance. This *Governance Handbook for Friends Schools* as well as its companion *Principles of Good Practice for Friends School Boards* together offer guidance and direction for those areas in which governance of Friends schools is unique.

The first 300 years of Friends education testify to the enduring relevance of the principles of Quakerism to the education of young people. In recent decades, our world has undergone paradigmatic changes in technology, finance, law, psychology, and neuroscience, to name just a few areas, all of which have had a direct impact upon the practice of education. This handbook acknowledges and embraces the new and dynamic contexts in which Friends schools operate in the twenty-first century, while re-affirming the appropriateness of Quaker-based decision making and other governance practices handed down from the Friends tradition. Here, it is valuable to note that the processes and practices in a Friends education are particularly relevant in these times where collaboration, listening skills, and empathy are in high demand for leaders of organizations, corporations and world political leadership.

■ *How can best use be made of this handbook?*

We encourage Friends schools to look to this handbook for a focused perspective regarding the peculiarly Quaker character of their school communities and related governance philosophy and practice. As each school is unique in its structure, challenges, and opportunities, this handbook should be understood as a guide rather than a definitive treatise on Friends school governance. It will serve its purpose if it stimulates thought, discussion, and review of current practices among those who have chosen the important service of overseeing the life and vision of Friends schools.

This handbook makes use of questions, mirroring the Quaker practice of using "*queries*." In the Quaker tradition, queries are broad questions that provide guidance and structure in engaging in open-minded and open-hearted examination of a specific area of concern. Good queries will stimulate thinking and discernment about their subject matter, hopefully leading into new or deeper understandings uniquely responsive to the lives of those using them.

Boards have often found it productive to use selected chapters of the *Governance Handbook for Friends Schools* in new trustee orientation and/or to study one chapter per board meeting, with discussion about that chapter as part of the meeting agenda. The intentional, ongoing study of this handbook will provide valuable opportunities for board development. This handbook is also a tremendous resource for helping to solve conundrums faced by leadership in a Friends school.

CHAPTER 1

Friends School Governance: An Overview

What is unique about a Friends school?

"Central to the mission of Friends education is the expectation that Friends schools will provide an academically sound education in a values-centered learning environment that is rooted in the faith and practice of Quakerism" (Cary, 1996). Four essential aspects distinguish Quaker education:

1) A firmly-held vision to be a Friends school by intentionally creating a Friends ethos in the on-going life of the school;

2) A board that is committed to the Quaker nature of the school, respecting and promoting the practice of Friends processes and testimonies;

3) Regularly held meeting for worship, and ongoing opportunities for members of the school community to grow in their understanding of the roots of Quakerism that inform school life;

4) Opportunities at all levels of the school to use a Quaker-based decision-making process and clarity about those times when this process will not be used.

In considering the question of what makes a Friends school unique, Paul Lacey, emeritus professor at Earlham College, has written about the "ethos and ethics" of Friends education. He writes of "an ethos of learning, of involvement, of care, and of hope." The ethos of a particular school is characterized by a

> . . . deeply-incised habit or character, stamped or imprinted into the institutional life and subsequently imprinted into the lives of those who are part of the institution . . . If there is, or can be, a spiritual unity in the aims of Friends education at every level, it would seem to manifest itself less in a single

comprehensive educational philosophy than in the creation of a particular kind of *atmosphere* or *climate* from which all aspects of school life — course-work, extra-curricular activities, and the interactions of students, staff, administration and faculty — take their form and meaning. Colin Bell has called this "the smell of the school" (Lacey, 1998).

Each Friends school draws strength from a meaningful relationship with the Religious Society of Friends. This relationship can take a variety of forms. The Friends Council on Education has developed numerous resources for Quaker renewal and growth, as well as membership criteria with queries to assess the Quaker dimension of a Friends school, which schools can use to embrace this relationship. (See www.friendscouncil.org.) Friends schools are encouraged to ensure a strong Quaker presence in the guidance of the school and encourage connections with Friends meetings where possible. Implicit in this encouragement is the assumption that Friends — individually and collectively — bring an experiential familiarity with Quaker process that is crucial to the proper functioning of a Friends school governing board.

In addition to formal indicators of Quaker identity, Friends schools that enjoy a care relationship with specific Friends Meeting(s) are wise to cultivate these relationships of mutual exchange, whereby members of both communities participate in each others' community life. (See *The Care Relationship*, a resource from the Friends Council on Education.)

▰ *What distinguishes governance authority in a Friends school from that of other schools?*

Governance implies direction, and direction implies authority. The authority of a Friends school board comes from the body that founded the school, which acted out of a spiritual leading grounded in pragmatism. This authority may be expressed in different ways. There may be a founding charter, or minutes of meetings, or articles and by-laws. A mission or vision statement and subsequent writings of the governing body often supplement these foundational documents. In its ongoing governance, the board of a Friends school looks to spiritual authority and the guidance that comes from the Light, appropriately channeled, of the many people who are involved with the school.

There are two faith-based qualities that can be said to distinguish Quaker governance from other models:

1. The first is a belief that there is a spiritual energy present in the world, often called the Light, and that we can choose to access this spiritual energy in the conduct of human affairs. Quakers believe that when we are open to the promptings of

this spiritual energy, our choices, decisions and our lives, both individually and institutionally, are better for it.

2. The second is a belief that each person is endowed with a measure of divine essence, often referred to as the Inner Light. So believing, Quakers have been very open to hearing divine guidance (truth), regardless of who was speaking it. The position or office of the speaker is much less important than what is being said. Quakers believe that there is a greater Light to be found among the many, than among the few, and so Quaker boards have generally been open to consulting widely, being mindful of different constituencies and voices, gathering as many perspectives as possible, before making decisions (Larrabee, 2002).

What is the role of Quaker practice in Friends school governance?

Because of the particular mission of Quaker education, and its historical and contemporary relationship to the Religious Society of Friends, it is crucial that a Friends school board learn about and then regularly remind itself of its Quaker roots and mission. In addition, the affairs of the Friends school board should be conducted with attention to Quaker-based decision making practice. (See Chapter 3.) Given that Friends school communities include and embrace people of all faiths and traditions, care should be taken to help those new to Friends education understand and feel comfortable with this practice.

Quakerism eschews both doctrine and dogma. However, Friends "testimonies" offer a set of guiding principles of conduct and intention, grounded in faith and in historical practice. (See Glossary and Reference sections.) While there are a large number of intentions and commitments that are widely shared among Quakers, six of the widely-practiced Friends testimonies may be easily called to mind with the acronym SPICES, which represents:

| Simplicity | Peace | Integrity | Community | Equality | Stewardship |

These Quaker "spices" provide a rubric within which the board can usefully consider its role in relation to school governance and the issues it considers. (See Chapters 2 and 7 for examples.) Similarly, the head of school may understand the daily operations of the school within this rubric, so that a Quaker ethos pervades each and every aspect of the school.

▪ What does it mean for a school to be in a "care relationship" with a Friends Meeting?

All Friends schools have the intention of acting from their Quaker missions, and are influenced by Quaker thought and practice. Many Friends schools, although not all, are in a care relationship with Friends Meetings (Monthly, Quarterly or Yearly Meetings). A Friends school may be considered to be in a care relationship with the Meeting that sponsored its founding or that continues to feel responsible for its spiritual and/or fiduciary well being. While this term originally indicated a relationship of direct oversight and control by the Meeting, it is currently used to describe a variety of configurations for responsibilities, roles, and connections between Friends schools and Friends Meetings.

Each school-Meeting relationship is unique in its care relationship, a function of its specific context and history. The diversity of relationships between Friends schools and Friends Meetings of all shapes, sizes and regions of the United States illustrates the heterogeneity of understandings that have developed around what it means for a school to be in a care relationship with a Friends Meeting. This is consistent with the Quaker tradition of not providing static answers and prescriptions, but instead offering a set of probing "queries" through which to engage in exploration and reflection. When the goal of the care relationship is for the meeting and school together to be continually open to new insight with fresh energy for revelation, and to be responsive rather than restrictive, then the relationship thrives. The evolution of Meeting-school care relationships is a continuing experiment, engaged for over 300 years with love and care-fullness. In the right relationship, the supporting community of Friends is a true partner with the school, and both partners commit to continuing growth with divine guidance. Both communities benefit enormously from the patient wisdom and loving care exercised through the relationship.

CHAPTER 2

Mission and Fiduciary Strength

■ *How is its mission especially significant for the board of a Friends school?*

As in independent schools generally, the mission of a Friends school should reflect the values-based philosophical intent of the school's founders, as well as the primary strategic direction of its governing board. The mission statement is a succinct expression of a school's unique purpose, its context of culture, values, and program, and its outreach to the community. It is the place where a school says, "This is what we strive for, this is what we believe in, this is why we are special."

Accordingly, the mission of a Friends school clearly articulates the commitment to cultivating the spiritual dimension of life, which is central to the aim of Quaker education. The mission of a Friends school is the basis for communicating the Quaker identity and ethos of the school. The mission supports an intention to create "a moral framework for the exercise of the knowledge that schools are created to impart" (Cary, 1996). In fulfilling its responsibility to promote the mission of the school, then, it is crucial that a board embrace the Quaker aspect of the mission as a "guidepost for all major decisions" (DeKuyper, 1998).

■ *What are the fiduciary responsibilities of the board as they relate to the mission?*

A school's Quaker character operates alongside of and in concert with the board's other mission priorities, most notably the financial. A concern for good stewardship — of land, buildings, and resources — has long been a priority of Quaker institutions. Given that Friends schools operate in the market-oriented context of independent schooling, there will be no mission to promote if the school board does not ensure the long-term financial success and stability of the institution.

> The mission/market tension cuts to the heart of board responsibilities in any non-profit and certainly so in a Friends school…The board must act as fiduciary for the institution's charitable assets, must be the trustee of *all* financial operations, and must specifically preserve and enhance the net assets (financial worth) of the enterprise. "No success, no survival" (Mueller, 2001).

Friends schools must be understood as businesses that call upon trustees to be careful stewards, not just of the dreams that led to their founding, but of their on-going budgetary needs as well. The board will be most effective when all board members have a clear, comprehensive grasp of the various sources of school income, the condition of investments and endowments, the annual budgets and financial statements (what they show and what they don't show), the accounting practices, the school's recent and past financial history, and the personnel policies that affect or are affected by the finances of the school.

How involved should the board be in financial management?

Sound financial management vitally supports the whole effectiveness of the school. A Friends school board must rightly concern itself with finances, as school budgets are roadmaps to institutional priorities. To do this well means that each and every trustee must make sure that s/he understands the overall financial picture and must not leave the job to only a few members of the board or staff. Ongoing dialogue between the board and the head (and, where appropriate, the business manager) nurtures a healthy collaborative partnership in this arena. Board members have a clear obligation to see that the financial condition of the school is reported accurately and completely at frequent intervals in a form that is readily understandable to the layperson. Accounts must be audited annually and good practice requires that those handling considerable sums of money should be bonded. In small school boards, this responsibility may be placed with the treasurer of the board in working with the head and/or business manager, and in larger school boards, this responsibility may be placed with the Finance Committee who works with the head and/or business manager to be sure that reliable financial practices are in place and accurate and usable financial records are kept.

Because of the passion Friends school board members feel for the mission, there may be a natural temptation for them to get overly involved in the day-to-day affairs of the school. However, for schools that have invested in strong professional administration, deeply detailed or too frequent board involvement in activities that are properly within the domain of "daily operations" or "management" can be a waste of board energy and a challenge to the effective collaborative relationship of board and head. Moreover, such involvement adds little value to the school. Governance expert and Harvard professor Richard Chait recommends that boards "become more like 'think tanks' characterized by 'strategic thinking' more so even than by 'strategic planning,' and focused on idea-generation and sorting, creating a legacy, image, and the like" (Bassett, 2002).

In fact, the most important job of the board, the job that cannot fully be done by faculty and staff, is to effectively engage in big picture strategic thinking — working to ensure the strength and sustainability of the school for generations to come. And in no area is this more important than in strategic financial thinking. Without a sufficient financial foundation, it will be impossible for the head and faculty (the school's educational experts) to carry out the vibrant educational program they are capable of providing.

In balancing the joint roles of fiduciary and keeper of the Friends school mission, the wisdom, expertise, and broad "outside" view of the board are especially needed in the areas of:

- Co-leadership with administration in the long-range planning of financial development, including multi-year budgeting;
- Co-participation with administration in defining, maintaining and enhancing the school's overall financial equilibrium in:
  - Educational programs and the human resources that implement them;
  - Capital plant;
  - Capital investment;
  - Capital development;
  - Enrollment management
- Co-development with administration of a sound, sustainable financial aid policy;
- Tuition setting — In the context of considering the areas listed above, the board is responsible to set a fair price for the school education.
- Collaboration with the head in creation of a policy with practical guidelines for collecting overdue and unpaid tuition.

What are the board's and head's roles in fiduciary planning?

The first essential is that the board and the head work closely together in all areas of planning for the mission-driven fiduciary health of the school. It is the board's responsibility to think and plan strategically, *in partnership with the head*, to ensure the long-term health and viability of the school. Then, when there are clear plans, it is the head's job, *while leading the faculty and staff,* to implement those plans. In sum, the head is an active participant in the board process and takes leadership for implementing plans that ensue.

■ *How and when should the board address budgeting and financial issues?*

Generally, the board reviews a financial statement at each board meeting. This current and accurate financial statement is a living guide for the board and the head. Some boards review an abbreviated summary statement each month and review a more detailed report each quarter. The time on the board meeting agenda for review of the financial statement, which reflects current income and expenses relative to the current year's budget, is the first step in budgeting for the upcoming year.

In many schools the budget is built with faculty and departmental input on needs, with priority lists constructed for review by the finance committee. Input for budget preparation also comes from

- the head, regarding program and staffing needs,
- the personnel committee, regarding proposed increases in salaries and benefits,
- the head and/or business manager, regarding plant maintenance needs,
- the head and/or development office, regarding annual giving and other fundraising expenses,
- the admission staff, for both tuition setting and enrollment management with expectation setting.

The admission and business offices of the school work with the head and board in considerations for the budget. The budgeting input process begins early in the fall with the goal of having the finance committee construct a balanced budget for presentation to the board. This will allow time for discussion and setting of tuition for the upcoming year, so that admissions and re-enrollment contracts can be sent out in a timely manner.

■ *What special considerations should a Friends school board make in setting tuition, financial aid, and salary budgets?*

A recurring budget tension occurs between the imperative for annual salary increases, the desire to keep tuition affordable, and the need for financial aid. It is important for the whole board to wrestle with the financial and mission issues inherent in this tension. The well-informed board will take into account historical patterns, current demographic trends, and mission imperatives in making sound projections for the school's future. In making decisions about rates of tuition, for example, it will be crucial to perform multiple-year projections, taking all variables into account and testing current proposals in the context of their long-term fiduciary impact.

Every Friends school board struggles with tuition, and for good reason. Commitment to the Friends testimonies of simplicity and equality may lead board members to want to set tuition as low as possible, thinking that this will make a Friends school education most accessible to people of all economic means. However, this is a potentially dangerous fallacy. Fred Calder, former head of Germantown Friends School and retired executive director of the New York State Association of Independent Schools, put it this way: "The central question for our schools is not whether we are elitist, but whether we care about other segments of society. The only way to be excellent — and bring *all* classes into our schools — is to charge what the upper echelons of the market [in the local area] can afford. Then everyone is served by quality, by fairness and by redistribution [through financial aid]. Those precious [financial aid] funds are not produced from low tuition" (Calder, 2000).

One way to think about a school's discretionary cash flow is with the metaphor of a three-legged stool, with the legs named: tuition, financial aid, and salaries. If one or two legs are out of proportion with the others, then a leg will have to be shortened or lengthened to keep the stool from tumbling over.

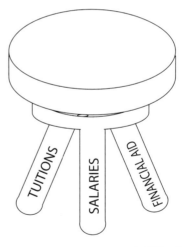

April Diop, 2002

If one leg reflects a commitment to keeping tuition as low as possible, and a second leg reflects having above-average levels of financial aid, then, unfortunately, the third leg follows from the other two: teachers are poorly paid (Ravdin, 2002).

Setting salary budgets is not just a fiscal decision; it is also very much a reflection of our religious testimonies. "The decision of what to pay those who labor in our religious and educational vineyards ought not to be separated from our testimonies about human justice and fairness. Friends school boards, therefore, must struggle not just with the demands of the marketplace in which they are operating, but also with the question of what is proper pay for those who serve the institution under their care. How one decides that matter is only partly a reflection of fiscal soundness; at its heart, it reflects the depth of our religious life" (Ravdin, 2002). As boards consider faculty salary, they must also attend to fair compensation for non-teaching staff. The board is responsible to care for all employees who labor long and hard hours to support the institution.

What other mission imperatives might be specific to Friends schools?

Below are some other examples of ways in which matters of school governance might be considered by the board through the "lens" of Friends testimonies of simplicity, peace, integrity, community, equality and stewardship (SPICES). These examples are not intended to be prescriptive nor exhaustive, but rather illustrative of this unique dimension of Friends school governance. (School names are fictional; examples are real.)

Simplicity — At Apple Blossom Friends School, we have developed a long-range plan that includes the creation of an alternative energy center, which will house our science department for all grades. The building will be powered by solar and wind-generated energy. Students and their families will learn about what it means to "live lightly on the earth."

Peace — At Cherry Harvest Friends School, we have endorsed a vision statement that embraces a whole-school approach to conflict resolution, expressed through our curriculum, pedagogy, parent education, and community service programs. As board members, we entrust the implementation of this vision to the head and her staff.

Integrity — In our small Willow Park Friends School, where board members wear multiple hats, those board members who are parents strive to think, discuss and discern from their board member role, temporarily setting aside their parent role. When matters come before us that might entail personal or financial conflicts of interest, we disclose the nature of those potential conflicts and offer to withdraw from consideration of such matters.

Community — At Walnut Valley Friends School, we place a priority on valuing diversity with regard to ethnicity, race, and sexual orientation in our admissions policy as well as in our recruitment and hiring policy, thereby giving concrete expression to our affirmation of the divine in all persons.

Equality — At Maple Shade Friends School, we have implemented a strategic plan for setting tuition, financial aid, and salary budgets, and we have emphasized congruent institutional and programmatic priorities, so that we remain accessible to people of all economic means, now and in the future.

Stewardship — At Beechnut Friends School, we review, on an annual and as-needed basis, investment policies, fundraising strategies, and physical plant priorities, so that they support the integrity of our mission, build for long-term financial sustainability, and affirm our social responsibility as citizens of the Earth.

What is the board's responsibility for school accreditation?

In Friends schools, just as in other independent schools, accreditation is the responsibility of the board of trustees. In some states a religious school does not technically need accreditation in order to operate, yet most Friends schools choose to obtain accreditation from their geographical and/or independent school accrediting body. The board is responsible to ensure that the school is accredited according to the state or regional association criteria and to ensure that recommendations from the accreditation evaluation are implemented faithfully and appropriately. The board may assign an ad hoc committee with related task forces to work with the accreditation process at periodic intervals. Once the review process is completed, the board and head are in charge of implementing final recommendations.

The Friends Council on Education is not an accrediting body; however, its board has established a set of queries for assessing the Quaker dimension of a Friends school, which it encourages all schools to use periodically to renew and revitalize the Quaker mission of the school.

CHAPTER 3

Decision Making

■ *What is the Quaker decision-making process?*

Early in the history of the Religious Society of Friends, Quakers recognized that conventional methods for making decisions tended to rely upon pre-existing power relationships and hierarchies, and failed to make room for divine guidance, the creative spirit moving among the group making a decision. Early Quakers believed that such methods failed to honor the Truth and potential gifts of many people. Accordingly, they developed new ways of making decisions that cultivated an active, communal search for Truth. This process requires each person to contribute input to a decision-making process according to his or her own experience of the Light, letting go of ego-driven convictions or opinions and listening hard for the wisdom that will emerge from the shared Light of the group.

In Friends Meetings and other Friends organizations, the decision-making process has a foundation in three beliefs:

- There is an aspect of divine creative spirit in every person;
- This creative essence can be accessed for guidance;
- Divinely inspired Truth hasn't all been handed down from the past, but continues to be revealed.

These beliefs, coupled with a set of attitudes and practices, create a worshipful context for all work and all relationships.

In Friends Meetings, all members have equal rights and responsibilities in decision making, and few formal roles exist. Members of the Meeting are equals. While some may show greater experience or more developed leadership, it is firmly believed that wisdom or inspiration may come from any person, and that the process of spirit-led dialogue allows greater wisdom to emerge from the group as a whole.

The Friends' goal in decision making is to seek spirit-led perspectives, to share insights courageously, and to listen openly to authentic concerns expressed by participants, finally discerning the "sense of the meeting," and confirming it by asking whether the group can unite with it. This process often gets translated as "consensus" outside of Friends communities, yet it is very different from secular consensus building. A "sense of the meeting" is a shared awareness of where spirit has led the group.

▮ *How does the Friends decision-making process work in a Quaker meeting for business?*

The protocol below for experiencing a highly ordered, participatory, effective Friends decision-making process was developed by the following Friends: Harry Hammond, Mary Wood, and Barbarajean Williams (2009) with the goal of providing guidance for Friends to experience the advantages of Friends decision-making process. The protocol is readily adaptable for use in Friends schools.

1. The clerk or a person she designates presents an item of business that is appropriate for the group and timely—not an announcement, not a report of information, but business that seems to require some action.

2. Next, members thoughtfully consider the subject that was introduced and, after being recognized by the clerk, make observations, share concerns, ask questions, etc.
   - The clerk provides some silence after each person speaks.
   - After the first speaker, those following express only views that have not already been voiced. Each speaks to the clerk and to the entire group.
   - The clerk may ask some to provide information or to say more.
   - This continues until all who want to speak have had the opportunity, or until the clerk senses that it's time to move on.

3. Now the clerk invites those whose ideas have changed — only those — to share their views.
   - During this time, it is not in good order for Friends to repeat or reinforce their own views, to debate or argue, or to repeat what others have already said.

4. Next, the clerk asks each person to reach (Friends might say "to turn toward the Light"), to discover a best answer or way forward. The only speakers at this point are those who are offering a new insight or a previously not seen way to address the issue.

- The clerk may want to provide a longer than usual space of silence in which members can wait and listen inwardly for a creative solution. Meanwhile, all involved free themselves of preconceptions, personality considerations, prejudices, and rigidities.
- As suggestions are made, the clerk may see a large area of agreement and will put that sense of the Meeting into words, as a tentative "minute." Some rewording of this may then be done with the help of others.

5. If the clerk senses that the group is ready to approve the minute, she or he will test that impression.
    - The clerk asks anyone who is uncomfortable with the minute to state what they cannot in good conscience agree to. If unity is not apparent, the clerk suggests a next step: hold the matter over ("seasoning") for the next meeting; refer the issue to an existing committee or appoint an ad hoc committee to engage in further discussion and/or research, and to bring back a recommendation or proposal. The clerk may also reframe the issue and schedule a non-decision-making threshing session.

What distinguishes decision making in a Friends school from that in a Friends Meeting?

Running a Friends school is an entirely different undertaking than living in a Quaker Meeting. Nonetheless, successful Friends schools heed their roots in Quaker faith and practice by maintaining structures and processes that include the thinking of students, faculty, parents, alumni/ae, and others in the decision-making matrix, to the extent that it is feasible.

> All Friends institutions, whether Friends Meetings or Friends schools, are rooted in the same concern: to do the business of the community with spiritual awareness, seeking to serve a larger, divine purpose by using methods and processes that help to bring this about. But doing business with spiritual awareness does not mean using the same processes regardless of the nature of the institution or the circumstances. In fact, perfunctory use of the same process in all circumstances quickly leads to human as well as spiritual exhaustion. Therefore, the clerk or a particular committee of a Friends Meeting is often given tasks to do, the authority with which to do them, and trusted with individual discernment, discretion and decision making on behalf of the whole community. Quaker Meetings could not function in a spiritually healthy way if they were to use a large group process in every situation.

The same is true for Friends schools. Many matters are delegated by the board to the head, and by the head to others, and it can well serve the spiritual vision of the school for these decisions to be made by the individuals to whom they are entrusted, or as they may consult with others. It is not good Friends process to involve the whole community in decisions that do not belong to the whole community (Larrabee, 2002).

The key is to be clear about which process is being used at any given time for any given decision. *The place where Friends schools often get into trouble is when they are not clear about which process is being used.* This could happen, for example, in a case where the head asks the faculty to consider a situation, without clearly delineating the decision-making process that will be followed, and faculty members think that they are being asked to make a decision. They do so, perhaps even using a spirit-led group process — later to find out that the head really only wanted their input. In this case, if the head makes a decision different from the faculty's decision, resentment and discord may ensue. This scenario could be remedied by the head clearly stating in advance what the intended decision-making process will be and what everyone's related roles will look like.

It may clear up some areas of confusion to note the differences that exist around decision making between Quaker Meetings and Friends schools, and between Friends schools and other independent schools. In a Quaker Meeting, decisions are jointly made, with all members having an equal say. However, in a Friends school, the decision-making structure is quite different. The board and the head hold final decision-making authority, dividing their responsibility across the spectrum of policy and operations. Going further, in Friends schools, often much more than in other independent schools and organizations, board and head frequently open the decision-making process to gather input widely. The perspectives of various members and constituency groups in the community are regularly sought. Since their help may be sought at any of these levels, members of the community are wise to ask for role clarity before entering into a process.

What are the benefits of Quaker-based decision making in a Friends school?

While good governance in a Friends school may be difficult at times, the benefits make the challenge worthwhile. "When all is said and done, the rewards of commitment to the process can be magnificent. There is a unified understanding of the work to be done, and a heightened sense of purpose. And there are not 'winners' and 'losers,' but a strengthened sense of a community that is joined in purpose and vision" (DiMicco, 2002). A reflection from a Friends school board and Meeting member illustrate this benefit:

> We recognize that misunderstanding and conflict are inevitable and potentially productive when dealt with thoughtfully. We have seen the value of building into

our ways of working frequent, systematic processes for low-risk and productive communication. The long period required for the coming to a sense of the meeting had a valuable result. From opposite stances we moved to a fusion of our views. I know personally that my original view changed, to be tempered by and to actually incorporate the views of others (Seaver, 2002).

Friends school educators confirm that commitment to good "Quaker process" often produces the seemingly paradoxical result of turning adversaries into partners. This outcome may be realized when participants let go of their personal agendas or desired outcomes, and open themselves up to the greater wisdom of the group, in worshipful consideration. The reward is likely to be solid, and ultimately quite satisfying. The key is *how* a decision gets made. If it gets made according to a deliberate process that is communicated in advance, and if everyone's voice in the decision-making group has an opportunity to be heard, then all participants will feel some ownership of the ultimate decision.

How can we use the Quaker-based decision-making process in a Friends school?

All decision-making groups in a school can be encouraged to use the concept of the Quaker-based decision-making process. The formal structure of this process requires the leadership of a facilitator, the clerk. (See Chapter 7 for a more detailed description of the role of the clerk.) This process requires the full participation of every member in the decision-making group — listening actively and attentively, as well as speaking. The process is based on the assumption that creative, spiritual energy ("that of God in everyone") is present in the decision-making group and is equally accessible by every member of the group. Therefore, the process requires active listening, reflection, and a commitment to reaching a decision with which all can unite — with the heart as well as the head.

Unity is not necessarily unanimity. A common misperception of Quaker business process is that a decision cannot go forward if one person decides to "stand in the way." The principle of unity does not give veto power to individual members of the community. One person cannot stand in the way of a decision made through a process of group unity. However, one person's Light may, indeed, help illuminate a path not initially seen by others. The perspective, question or concern that one person contributes to the dialogue may influence the decision of the group and may modify the proposed action before it moves forward. Expressed reservations may influence the group in deciding not to move forward until further research is conducted on the issue. The group may also decide to take additional time for a process of reflection in order to understand, assimilate, and incorporate the truth in the perspective of one of its members.

A Quaker-based decision-making process requires commitment from all members involved. The necessary inward stance of each group member is "one of patience, openness, humility, and teachability" (Grundy, 2002). Barbara Caldwell (1998) describes the commitments required for each group member as including:

- Open-mindedness and a willingness to change one's mind;
- A willingness to surrender pre-conceptions, ideological principles and dearly held beliefs to the wisdom of the group;
- An understanding that this process takes time;
- Trust in and respect for the deciding group and the process;
- An understanding that the group is wiser than any one individual;
- A willingness to hear each person's views without prejudice;
- A willingness to contain reactive emotion (e.g. fear, anger, irritation) while focusing on the work task at hand;
- Acknowledgement that there is a creative spiritual source to which we may turn as we make decisions;
- Patience and the ability to use silence constructively.

While this process is uniquely Quaker, there is research in corporate America that suggests this kind of group involvement also builds better team leadership and better outcomes. The corporate term "distributed leadership" is in essence at the heart of all Quaker process. Quaker discernment and group involvement are radically current.

What is the role of a leader in using the Quaker-based decision-making process in a Friends school?

Nancy van Arkel describes the relationship between effective leadership and careful discernment in the following discussion, prepared for the Institute for Engaging Leadership in Friends Schools (2006). Friends are often ambivalent about leadership. This does not need to be the case in Friends schools, if the decision-making work is grounded in the Friends process. Five aspects of Friends decision-making process inform good leadership in Friends schools:

- Openness to seeking Truth
- Trust in the wisdom of the group
- Active and transparent discernment
- Discipline in attending to good practices
- Awareness of spiritual presence and assistance

Effective leadership (head, division director, committee clerk, board clerk, faculty leader, student leader, parent leader) in Friends schools is closely tied to discernment. The group already knows, on some level, what is needed to move forward; however, groups, like amoebas, can have difficulty doing more than oozing first in one direction and then another. The role of the leader is to listen deeply on both a spiritual and a practical level, and to gather the collective sense of Truth in a particular matter. The leader facilitates the transformation of that corporate sense into a concrete set of action steps and maintains the focus of the group through to the desired outcome. The authority of the leader in this process derives from two sources — what the group gives and what the leader is willing to claim. The group empowers the leader to act on its behalf. While leadership skills and institutional knowledge are important, it is essential that the group trust its leaders to value the process of seeking discernment and to value the collective wisdom. Without that trust, the leader will be powerless to serve the group effectively.

The leader must fully accept the obligations of the leadership role. Ambivalence about claiming the authority that has been bestowed by the group and the institution is an abuse of the trust that has been placed in the leader. Claiming authority means a willingness to:

- focus the energy of the group towards a specific goal,
- keep the group from unnecessary distractions,
- remind the group of its success along the way,
- acknowledge the brutal truths of the organization,
- be a spokesperson, cheerleader, disciplinarian, counselor, and organizer,
- take personal risks to benefit the whole,
- be disciplined, while also maintaining an openness to new truths.

Who makes decisions in a Friends school?

Unlike Quaker Meetings, Friends schools have a hierarchy of decision making and decision makers that arises from the permanent roles and responsibilities of the members of these communities (e.g., head of school, admissions director, school nurse, classroom teacher, board member). The realities of operating a school — including time constraints, business issues, managing operations that include many people from diverse perspectives, and more — necessitate that decision making take multiple forms, including forms that are different from those used in Quaker Meetings. However, in both Quaker Meetings and Friends schools, decision-making processes are structured so that the spirit, as much as possible, guides discussion and deliberation.

In a Friends school, groups and individuals have differing responsibilities for making decisions. Decisions may be made:

- Alone, by one individual who has the authority and responsibility for the decision;
- Alone, with the input of those who will be directly affected by the decision;
- As equal partners with those whom the decision will affect (which most closely resembles the equal partnership of members in a Friends Meeting);
- By delegating the decision to those who will be directly affected by the decision (Edstene, 1996).

What decisions are the responsibility of the board in a Friends school?

Important policy decisions are the responsibility of the board. Important policies are those that ensure the school's well being, particularly in the long-term. These include the mission statement, admissions policy, hiring policy, financial aid policy, personnel policy, anti-discrimination policy, conflict of interest policy, whistle-blower policy, financial management and investment policies, insurance policies, sexual harassment policy, drug and alcohol policy, and policy-related plans, such as a crisis management plan, and a strategic plan.

It is useful for the recording clerk to maintain a separate policy book for the board and to highlight policy statements in copies of the minutes. Otherwise, outdated policies may remain on the books, or good work may be lost as trustees rotate off the board. Having a policy book is essential for the orientation of new board members. Trustees are responsible for ensuring that school policies are in keeping with the school's mission and values.

It is essential that the board and head be clear about their approval authority in school-related decisions. This will vary school to school, and will be in constant evolution in any one school, but begins with specifying which decisions the head will make and which decisions will be made by the board. But clarity doesn't stop here. It is important to determine when the head (making the final decision) would be expected to consult with the board prior to making it. Additionally, it will be of use to know which decisions the board would like to be informed of by the head. Being clear in advance about all of these things will make for much smoother school operation.

Decision Making

In practice, most decisions are shared by the board and head, with some being made by the board (with the head's input), some shared equally, and some made by the head (with the board's input):

Focus	Decision-Making Authority
Mission By-Laws Conflict of Interest Policy Investment Policy Admissions & Financial Aid Policies Personnel & Hiring Policies	Board Decisions Head's Input*
Spiritual Dimension of the School Development Plan Strategic Plan Sexual Harassment Policy Drug and Alcohol Policy Crisis Management Plan	Collaborative Decisions: Board and Head
Implementation of Board Policies Daily Operational Systems Curriculum & Instruction Hiring & Evaluating Staff Parent Relations Facilities Management	Board's Input* Head's Decisions*

* Note: head's decisions and input may incorporate input from faculty and staff

FCE/PYM 2002

CHAPTER 4

Roles and Responsibilities

How can we develop a clear understanding of roles, responsibilities, and inclusivity, especially as these relate to decision making in a Friends school?

Particularly because of the ideal of equality in Quaker decision making, people involved in Friends school communities are frequently under the misunderstanding that each and every decision ought to be made by consensus. A common statement of frustration is: "If this is a Quaker school, why wasn't my voice involved in that decision?" While school community members do understand that certain routine decisions do not require full participation in decision making, there is often little agreement beyond that, and even small decisions can seem to take on large import in a community that has not clarified decision-making processes. It is very important, therefore, for the board and the head of school to clarify levels of participation and responsibility in decision making — in overall principle and before specific new decisions are undertaken.

In terms of decision making authority, roles, and responsibility, a Friends school community is not a community of equals, as some groups or individuals have more authority, responsibility, and decision-making duties than others do, depending on the context for each decision. It is important that groups and individuals within a school community know the limits of their decision-making authority, so they do not feel mistreated when they reach a decision, which is later overturned or revised by a higher authority. In a Friends school, the ideal within the testimony of equality can best be put into action by the respect that is given to the contributions of the various constituencies, and by taking care to have consultation with affected constituencies built into every decision.

All involved in a school community (including those alive who are no longer directly involved) are stakeholders. Their voices are needed and attended to. However, the trustees are the key *shareholders.* They need to take into account those who will be involved in the future, as well as those in the larger community who will be impacted by current and future developments at the school. Thus, the role of trustee, at times, is to be "weighty" in a way that may seem not responsive-enough to the voices of those currently involved (such voices often being concerned more with personal and short-term interests). Heads may find it difficult to be weighty in that way, especially when there is the potential to confuse their own welfare with the welfare of the school. Trustees represent the future, not only today's and yesterday's constituents (Hammond, 2002).

In creating and reviewing policy, one common practice is to seek input from the persons who are subject to or who will implement that policy, as well as from experts in the field and from other schools. For an important decision, the board should clarify roles and responsibilities with each constituency (students, faculty, parents, administrative team, alumni, Meeting) at the start of a decision-making process, so each person and group knows that a decision is being made and who the accountable decision makers will be. In a Quaker context, this clarification may be termed, "Who is the Meeting?" This phrase addresses the question of who are the members of the designated group directly involved in making the decision.

There are actually two guiding questions regarding participation in the decision-making process:
- Whose voices need to be heard on this issue?
- Whose voices must be part of the actual decision-making group?

In defining the decision-making process, it is important for various constituents who are not the accountable decision makers to know if they will be consulted or informed regarding the decision. In many cases, after a preliminary decision has been reached, the head or the board or both in collaboration will be called upon for final approval.

Responsibility Charting Exercise
It is often productive for a board to complete a "Responsibility Charting" exercise to clarify roles and responsibilities before making decisions in major areas of school business. This may be a useful exercise to engage in before a complex

matter is tackled. Alternatively, the responsibility charting tool can be scheduled several times a year, with different hypothetical examples, as a board development activity.

When using this rubric at a board meeting or retreat, it is common to find differences in perspective on who has or "should have" decision-making authority and responsibility in each area. These differences are the treasure unearthed by the tool. The value in doing this exercise lies less in establishing permanent "right answers" (as right answers may change over time) and more in developing the thinking and shared perspective of board members.

To use the sample rubric below, consider a decision to be made (using a hypothetical decision from the sheet provided or insert one of your own). Then ask:
- Who has approval-level authority for this decision?
- Who has responsibility to carry out the decision?
- Who would be consulted for input before the decision is made?
- Who would need to be informed of the decision's outcome?
- Who wouldn't be involved at all?

APPROVAL: This level is the person or group accountable for the final approval of a decision and the final accountability of a project.

RESPONSIBLE: This is the person or group who takes the project through to completion, from beginning to end. This level has oversight of the complete process and/or project, related tasks and decision-making responsibilities, and is accountable if no action takes place.

CONSULTED: This is the person or group who is consulted for input prior to the decision being made. This person or group does not have power to change or stop the decision; however, they are accountable for giving their best input. They are often consulted for input based on experiential expertise, or for reasons of inclusiveness, tactful consideration, and multiple systemic perspectives.

INFORMED: This person or group is told about the decision or project. They do not have input, although they need to be informed of the outcome. They may also be informed prior to decision making, so they are aware that a decision is being made or a project is being initiated and they know their level of involvement in the process.

RESPONSIBILITY CHARTING FOR DECISION MAKING

The decisions to...	Board Officers		Board Mem	Board Cttee	Whole Board	Head	Parent	Fac/ Staff	Alums	Meeting	
	Clerk	Treas.									
Admit a student											
Change the math curriculum											
Revise the mission of school											
Approve the budget											
Launch a capital campaign for endowment											
Increase annual giving by 10%											
Change the contracts for maintenance of property											
Change investment policy											
Hire new faculty from search committee recs											

Adapted from the Center for Applied Research, 1997

A = Approval   R = Responsible   C = Consulted   I = Informed
? = don't know   0 = not applicable

Blank copies of the responsibility chart may be downloaded from the website of the Friends Council on Education > Resources > Governance Tools.

■ *Does the board focus on policy and the head on operations?*

For many years, this has been the standard wisdom. However, governance specialists (Carver & Carver, 1997) now point out that it is often difficult to fully separate these two areas of focus. It is clear that trustees need to know something about operations to make sound policy decisions; similarly, good operational decisions by the head are founded in a solid knowledge of relevant policies. Both operational and policy decisions are made each day — even the assistant teacher on recess duty, who says, "You can't ride a skateboard on the playground" is making a policy decision at a certain level. A large grey area exists where policy and operational matters overlap. In fact, it's rare that a decision belongs entirely in one camp or the other. However, despite this, it remains critical to pay attention to these distinctions.

The important thing is that the board is responsible (at the highest, approval level) for long-term policy decisions and decisions that affect the long-term health and viability of the school. To make those decisions, the board must know something about operations, but it does not, as a rule, make operations-level decisions. Working in the complementary role, the head has approval-level charge for making operations-level decisions and short-term policy decisions that allow for the smooth running of operations. The head is also charged with participating in the long-term policy-related thinking of the board — in fact it cannot happen effectively without the head — but the head is not finally responsible for these decisions.

The key element in these matters is communication. It is a valuable practice for boards and heads to engage in continual questioning and negotiating, asking each time a matter comes up for decision: Is this primarily a policy-level decision? Is it primarily operational? With clarity in hand, board and head may consciously decide to verge over the "line" and engage in, for instance, a policy discussion that is enriched by reviewing operational standards — with the fore-knowledge and consent of the head. Or the head may request the board's input or feedback on an operational matter, which the board may agree to do because sound operations affect the long-term health and viability of the school — again, making a conscious decision to step over the traditional boundary for a specific (and time-delimited) purpose.

Who has the ultimate leadership role — the head or the board?

We may think, in very rough terms, of three models of school leadership:
1. the head in front, guiding and motivating the board,
2. the board in front, leading and directing the head,
3. a full partnership, where both work in tandem in a well-understood and highly articulated system, informed and enhanced by each others' different viewpoints and roles.

All three models have their time and place. For instance, a founding head may have a very strong role in the first years of a new school's life, especially if many board members are new to their roles. Conversely, a board may find itself doing more guiding and instructing with a new, as-yet-inexperienced head. Both of these patterns can be highly functional in the life of the school and will probably be transitional. The third pattern is the one to aim for in the long term, with mature board and head working in partnership. Here they're joined at equal leadership strength in their distinct roles, in full communication, carrying the weight across clear, oft-negotiated, and well-differentiated lines of responsibility.

▪ *How can the board ensure that it is staying within its role?*

When a board is troubled by having become heavily engaged in one or more operational matters, it is wise to ask:

- Have we provided sufficient training in best practices for board work?
- Are we getting clarity on roles, responsibilities, and boundaries before engaging in discussion and decision making on the board?
- Do we check with the head before involving ourselves in anything operational?
- Do we have enough high-level, meaningful work for the board to discuss and do?
- Are we making full use of trustees' skills and capacities? (Are board members bored?)
- In the case of a relatively new school: Are we ready to move on from being an organizing board (by necessity more involved in operations)? Are we ready to pull back and take on the long-range perspectives and habits of behavior of a governing board?

One Friends school board uses a handy method to make the policy vs. operations topic visible and regularly evaluate their performance with it. Board members complete a postcard-size evaluation (shown at right) at the close of each meeting and deliver the results at the start of the next one. They note that there are "correct" answers to the first two questions, but on the third they feel they may justifiably decide to move their focus to the operational side — although only with conscious intent. Board members report that answering these questions regularly raises everyone's consciousness about the quality of board discussion and that productive behavior has steadily increased since the implementation of this method. (An electronic copy of the form can be found on the website of the Friends Council on Education for your use: Resources > Governance Tools.)

The issues covered today were:

Trivial   1   2   3   4   5   Essential

The materials provided were:

Worthless   1   2   3   4   5   Indispensable

Today's discussion concerned primarily:

Operations   1   2   3   4   5   Policy, strategy, idea generation

COMMENTS:

(Adapted from Greene Street Friends School, 2007)

CHAPTER 5

Shared Vision and Strategic Planning

What is the significance of a shared vision in a Friends school?

In a Friends school, the "visioning" process draws from the deep, spiritual purpose of the school's founding, and from the school's enduring mission, in order to assure the school's continuing integrity and viability. The spirit-led imagination, intuition, dreams and discernment of all constituencies involved in the school's past and present come together to create a shared vision for the future. The board of a Friends school is responsible to engage itself and the school community in a process of creative, participatory visioning of the school's future on a regular basis (usually every five to ten years).

A shared vision in a Friends school is one that has evolved from a process of corporate discernment, similar to the Quaker process of shared decision making. Rich resources for creating a shared vision are provided by the perspectives of all constituencies in the school's internal and external communities: from members of the board, head, administrators, faculty, parents, students, alumni/ae, Meeting members, to heads from other local schools and organizations, and other community leaders. Accordingly, the resulting vision belongs to the whole community, not any particular individual or group. As organizational theorist Peter Senge has written, "At the heart of building shared vision is the task of designing and evolving ongoing processes in which people at every level of the organization, in every role, can speak from the heart about what really matters to them, and be heard" (Senge et al, 1994).

Specific goals for the school's future emerge and become clarified during the visioning process. Indeed, a shared vision provides solid ground for decision making, because it has evolved through such a careful, open, challenging, thoughtful, and heartfelt process, and because it has engaged a sense of personal "ownership" by a broad cross-section of the school community. Decision making that is built on this strong foundation echoes the Quaker testimony of good stewardship, which calls for our investment of time and money in sustainable and renewable resources and in work that supports our values and beliefs. In many ways, the Friends testimony on stewardship resonates with the tradition of the Six Nations Iroquois Confederacy for making decisions with a vision of the "seventh generation," i.e., for those who will inherit the consequences of our decisions long after we are gone.

■ *How does shared vision inform the strategic plan for a Friends school?*

A shared vision provides the foundation for the strategic planning process and the ongoing success of the school. Strategic planning is the tool that allows a Friends school board to fulfill its dual responsibility: to safeguard its mission, and to implement a vision for the school's healthy and vibrant future. While the visioning process engages each board member's heart, spirit, and creativity, the strategic planning process demands each board member's capacity for *discernment*. Discernment, in the Quaker sense of the term, is a precursor to decision making. It rests upon a willingness to patiently listen for Truth, in oneself and in others. It requires intellectual, emotional, and spiritual attention and engagement.

As non-public entities, Friends schools operate within the context of their own chosen missions, as well as within the competitive context of independent schooling. This tension between "market-driven" and "mission-driven" imperatives places a particular burden upon Friends schools. They must compete successfully in the educational marketplace, while also providing a quality education within a framework that embraces the testimonies of the Religious Society of Friends. This formidable board responsibility and task load is made manageable through the design and direction of a strategic plan, which serves as a map that all will use to make their way through the continually evolving future of market-driven and mission-driven deliberations.

The strategic plan, which moves from the current condition of the school to the future condition of the school, transforms the school's vision into goals with measurable objectives and action steps. It is best created for a particular time frame, such as three to five years from the present.

How does a Friends school board engage in strategic planning?

The strategic planning process draws on the very best aspects of Quaker process. It is a participatory and creative process of discernment conducted in a values-centered context. The process usually consists of multiple interrelated phases, which may be expressed uniquely school by school. The example below illustrates six typical planning phases.

PHASE 1 — Steering Committee or Ad Hoc Strategic Planning Committee
A steering committee, appointed by the board and led by a board member, best leads the entire strategic planning process. This committee organizes and coordinates the work of the planning process, and includes the head, the board clerk, and some or all of the clerks of the task forces that will be described in Phase 3, below. It is wise for the board to consider engaging a professional consultant for guidance. Excellent use can be made, as well, of the many resources that exist on strategic planning for independent schools and non-profit organizations. (These are listed in the Resources section of this handbook.)

PHASE 2 — Mission
The planning process begins with a careful review of the school's mission. This is usually structured in a broad, highly participatory format that allows all stakeholders to "own" the mission statement as an essential part of the life of the school. Reviewing the mission may result in wholesale change or a subtle refinement that is more in keeping with the school's Quaker identity and ethos.

PHASE 3 — Information Gathering
The next phase of the process is to gather information from as many constituents in the school community as possible — building shared vision as you go. Surveys, focus groups, and retreats with community members representative of various school constituency groups, as well as external community representatives are the most common tools used to find out what community members feel are the essential enduring values of the school (values that may be enhanced and that can be used successfully for marking purposes) and what their fondest wishes are for bringing the school to its highest potential.

Essential to the plan's eventual implementation is the enthusiastic participation of the faculty and the staff. Therefore, it is important that faculty and staff are integrally involved throughout the process. Often schools include parents, Meeting members, alums, and other important external community members. Students may be included in this phase, as appropriate.

From the information-gathering process, essential needs for a thriving and sustainable future at the school will emerge. The steering committee will write focusing questions, aimed at discovering how to provide for these needs, which will direct the work of each task force.

PHASE 4 — Task Forces or Work Groups

Here is where the real work of the strategic planning process occurs. The steering committee reviews the information-gathering input to see what themes exist in order to propose initiatives to the board. When the board has formulated the strategic initiatives, task forces are set up to develop objectives and action steps. Task forces are composed of board members and staff, joined by highly trained and capable people from across and beyond the school community. Existing committees of the board may be authorized to work on specific goals, objectives and action steps, and may add several ad hoc members for this purpose. They take up their focusing questions and set to work researching, analyzing, and finally crafting far-thinking and sometimes out-of-the-box recommendations to answer them.

In this phase of strategic planning, a particular tool for discernment called Force Field Analysis can be valuably employed by each Task Force (Agazarian, 2000). Implementing force field analysis involves looking at the driving and restraining forces that may support or hinder achievement of each goal. The task force brainstorms using the following questions:
- What forces are in place in the school community and/or the external environment that are driving forces toward the goal of this initiative?
- What forces are in place in the school community and/or the external environment that are restraining forces against achieving the goal of this initiative?

The key analysis is in looking at the restraining forces to see if there are themes or clusters of forces working together, and how these forces might be modified (if at all). Choosing the forces that can be modified is a first step in generating action steps for the strategic plan. In the example below, the action steps were developed by a work group looking at the restraining force of "not enough time for board development."

PHASE 5 — Documenting the Plan

The phase involves shaping the working documents in order to implement the plan and publicizing the goals and major objectives of the strategic plan to the school community and to the wider community. In this phase, the steering committee can create the following documents:
1. A compilation of all task force recommendations
2. A short list of five – seven key strategic goals distilled from the recommendations, used to publicize the good news of the strategic plan to the whole community

3. A set of spreadsheets, one for each key strategic goal, that list all the action steps to be taken over the next five years to accomplish the goals. These spreadsheets also include who will be responsible for each action step, time and resources needed, and evaluation information. The spreadsheets are the workhorse of the strategic plan; without them, the plan cannot be implemented.
4. A clear process outlining the responsibility for yearly implementation, evaluation and adaptation.

A sample spreadsheet might look like this:

GOAL: To provide an ongoing program of professional development to our board.							
Action Step	Date Initiated	Responsible Person/Group	Proposed Budget	Human Resources	Date Evaluated	Evaluating Person/Group	
Establish annual board retreat	June 2010	Executive Committee	$1,500	Outside facilitator	One month after retreat	Whole board	
Develop annual board orientation	August 2011	Governance Committee	0	Host and organizer	Annual board evaluation	New trustees and mentors	
Regularly study and discuss FCE and NAIS Governance Handbooks	September 2010	Governance Committee	$500	Whole board	Annual board evaluation	Whole board	
Etc.							

PHASE 6 — Implementation

The final phase of strategic planning is to implement the plan. To do this, board leadership with the head of school reviews the strategic plan documents each spring or summer in order to lift up the work that will be targeted for the coming year. Tasks are parceled out to individual board committees, and to staff, who then incorporate them into their action plans for the months ahead. At the end of the year, each committee reviews its progress, submits a short report to the full board, and the process begins anew for the coming year. The strategic planning document is not etched in stone, but rather a guide for action and reflection on that action. The action steps may be modified according to changing internal and external conditions, which is why an annual evaluation process is important.

CHAPTER 6

Advancement

What is the work of the board in building a strong foundation for fundraising and marketing in a Friends school?

This chapter supplements the discussion about the board's fiduciary responsibility that can be found in Chapter 2. Here, the major responsibility of the board for financial oversight and accountability is extended into the areas of fundraising and marketing.

Board members in Friends schools are stewards for the school's resources, both short-term and long-term. Dedicating substantial time at a board meeting for reflection on the Friends testimony on stewardship and its relevance to the work of the board in assuring the viable longevity of the school sets a valuable context for board members' ongoing involvement in fundraising and marketing. The long-term viability of the school depends not only on the board's sound financial management of the school's resources, but also the board's visionary and vigorous leadership in fundraising and marketing.

The board of a Friends school is responsible for ensuring that the school has adequate resources and that resources are effectively managed. Even though fundraising activities, such as grant writing and special events, are often initiated and carried out by staff and/or parent volunteers, the board is responsible for making sure that the school has enough resources to carry out its mission.

Board members are responsible for providing enthusiastic leadership in fundraising by articulating the mission of the school and building the case for others to give substantial resources to the school. Board members are expected to participate directly in fundraising by attending special events, making solicitations — particularly for the annual fund, for planned giving, and during capital campaigns — and by making contacts and networking on an ongoing basis with potential donors to the school.

Similarly, board members are charged with ensuring that the school has an effective plan for getting its message out to all current and potential constituents. The board is instrumental in making sure that the school is able to market itself in such a way that sufficient enrollment comes through the door and that positive public perception has been created, without which successful fundraising work will be severely hampered.

In all of this work, board members are carrying the school forward by articulating its strengths to others, by demonstrating their passion for the mission and vision of the school, and by showing their good will in engaging others in the privilege and opportunity to support the school — whether it be through enrolling their children, sharing in the good news of a strong school reputation, or making important financial contributions.

How are individual board members in a Friends school involved in the work of fundraising?

Individual board members are the models for contributing personal financial resources to the school. It is essential to have full board participation at a challenge level in annual giving. One hundred percent board giving to the annual fund and to capital campaigns demonstrates the board's leadership and commitment to the school's mission. Board members give generously to the school, according to their individual capacities for giving. There is a traditional saying about the three Ws: a board member is chosen for her/his work, wisdom, and wealth. Although wealth is a relative concept, it is important for board members to support the school with financial resources (in keeping with their individual capacities) in addition to time, energy, and enthusiasm.

Friends have a long-standing commitment to building socially useful institutions on financially solid ground. Many contemporary Quakers are, by nature, "thrifty," and bring to their work on a board a concern about consumerism and materialism. This concern may, at first, create a dynamic tension with the goal of fundraising. This tension can be gracefully productive when the bigger picture of the school's transformative mission and the need for stable fiscal health are kept as the focus.

How does the fundraising culture and practice of the school strengthen the school's identity as a Friends school?

Raising money to support the school is an essential mission in itself. The fundraising mission cannot be separated from the guiding mission of a Friends school, and must be bold enough to support facilities and academic programs at a level of excellence commensurate with the school's mission and vision. The board is responsible for generating revenues through philanthropic means to sustain and strengthen the programs of the school, including the values-based curriculum and the ongoing orientation of students, families, faculty and board members to Quaker spiritual values in Friends education.

The following queries may serve the board in ensuring that all aspects of fundraising for the school reflect the school's core Quaker commitments:

How can we ensure that all fundraising work and activities are carried out with integrity?

How is stewardship exercised in the use of social and material resources for fundraising?

How do the fundraising activities promote fellowship and community building for the school community?

How can we celebrate all of the gifts (large, small, and in-kind) that support the ongoing operation of the school?

Have all Quaker and Quaker-affiliated resources for funding been carefully explored?

Are all donors treated with sensitivity and respectful gratitude?

Are all gifts carefully acknowledged and accurately accounted for?

How are gifts reported to the community in sensitive and celebratory ways?

Is endowment growth prioritized to assure the future health of the school as a Friends school?

Do we have a balanced focus on fundraising efforts that will net substantial sums over time (Annual Giving, Planned Giving, Capital Campaigns)?

Are we all setting ourselves to the work of careful cultivation of loyal donors, work that will be necessary to achieve these substantial financial goals?

How is the language used in fundraising publications and conversations consistent with the school's mission statement and core Quaker commitments?

How are the people involved in fundraising (volunteers and staff) recognized, thanked and carefully monitored to avoid burnout?

Are fundraising events well coordinated and carefully scheduled in order to avoid donor fatigue and volunteer burnout?

Is there a healthy balance between staff and volunteer activity for fundraising and are the roles and responsibilities of each person/group clear?

How do Friends testimonies and advices serve as a guide for fundraising activities and investment policies?

▪ What are some common challenges for Friends school board members' work in fundraising?

CHALLENGE #1: Not understanding the true cost of education

"This is a private school that charges a hefty tuition. Why does it need additional funds?" This is a common question asked by those who are new to the work of nonpublic, nonprofit schools. The board's responsibility for development includes educating the school's constituencies and the outside community about the fact that tuition covers only a portion of the true cost of educating each student, and that, with tuition alone, we cannot build financial security for the school's future growth and success. It is not wise for a school budget to be based solely on tuition income, as enrollment will naturally fluctuate. Establishing and carefully managing sources of income beyond tuition is a key responsibility of the board. These additional income sources may include the annual campaign, endowment income, grants, bequests and other planned giving gifts, donations of goods and services, and special event income. Overall, solicitation of major donors generates the best foundation for funding Friends schools.

CHALLENGE #2: Potential conflict with Quaker testimonies

In a Friends school, consideration must be given to possible challenges inherent in traditional fundraising events and activities. For example, the Religious Society of Friends continues to bear testimony against betting, gambling, lotteries, and other endeavors to receive material gain without equivalent exchange. Friends school boards must, therefore, wrestle with decisions about raffles and lotteries. Many Yearly Meetings of the Religious Society of Friends hold strong testimonies against any use of tobacco or alcohol; others counsel moderation. Again, Friends school boards must consider policies about alcohol use at fundraising events where alcoholic beverages might traditionally be served. Each Friends school's board should engage in discussion of these Friends testimonies and how they might affect the fundraising culture of the school.

CHALLENGE #3: Personal aversion to fundraising

Individual board members may have their own personal aversions to fundraising. Board members must assess their own barriers to involvement in development and fundraising. Adding additional fundraising activities will not accomplish the goal of raising funds for the school, if the board members' aversions to fundraising are not addressed. Typical challenges include board members' feelings that they don't know how to raise money, that they don't have time to raise money, and that they don't have any useful contacts for fundraising. This is where a board retreat on fundraising and development might be useful. It is also useful for the board to enlist the services of a consultant to train board members, so that they may become more skilled at and more comfortable with cultivation and solicitation.

How are board members in a Friends school involved in the work of marketing?

Generally, a Friends school will create a marketing plan to focus its outreach work, either using internal resources (staff, board members, parents, etc.) or the services of an outside consultant. The planning process might well begin with a survey of local opinion leaders to find out how well the school is known in the local community and what it is known for. This may be accompanied by focus group and/or survey inquiry into how parents and others closely connected with the school see it.

From this data, a school can know if its strengths are sufficiently known in the community, or if a marketing campaign will be useful in raising its reputation and bringing in new students and families. Additionally, the data will be used to create a short list of key values that the head, administrators, board members, and others will highlight in presentations, newsletters, notes to parents, etc. The idea is to get the message across by focusing attention on a few key messages, strong core messages that can advance public awareness of the mission and vision of the school.

Often in the data gathering for marketing, issues are identified which need further work — for instance, a perception that the school is not committed to athletics — and the board must wrestle with a conversation about this matter to better understand the perceptions and whether there are kernels of truth in the data findings. Further, these sorts of undertakings often tease up a conversation about honest "advertising and promotion" of the school's strengths — and board members need to provide leadership as the school works to get clear on its messages as well as to discern whether negative feedback is fair — or if, the school might pay more attention to the area of concern (Hoerle, 2009).

Board members can be instrumental in proposing and helping to create a marketing plan. Once it's in place, they can make a real difference by actively supporting it through promoting the core messages at every opportunity.

CHAPTER 7

Effective Board Process

■ What does effective board/committee process look like in Friends school governance?

In a Friends school, as in most other schools, the board focuses on bringing to life its shared vision of the school's future. Toward that end, the board makes policy decisions, builds a sound financial foundation for the school's operation and growth, hires the head, and nurtures relationships among all parts of the greater school community, including the Meeting, families, faculty, staff, head, the board itself, and the surrounding community.

There is another dimension of effective board process, unique to Friends' boards, which merits special attention here. Namely, members — and especially the board clerk — need to feel comfortable with and grounded in Quaker decision-making process. The clerk does not need to be a Quaker; however, it is important for the clerk be open both to understanding the Quaker-based business meeting practice that is used in Friends business meeting, and to leading the board in a manner informed by that practice. (See Chapter 3 for a detailed description of this practice.)

■ How do openness, confidentiality, and trust factor into the work of a Friends school board?

Board effectiveness requires an understanding of the right balance between openness and confidentiality. Trust is a natural outgrowth of finding this balance. In a climate of mutual trust, a board will find that its capacity to work together, as a whole, will prosper. Trust cannot be hurried or forced; rather, it develops over time — in the group and within individuals — in response to the lived experience of consideration and care.

Key to building and maintaining trust is having a clear understanding of the need for confidentiality within each decision-making group and in all parts of the board's work. For example, in the course of an ordinary year, board members may be called upon to consider sensitive personnel matters related to employment or compensation; they may need to hold knowledge of fellow board members' opinions and positions for weeks or months about issues that may be hotly debated; and they may need to be apprised of delicate matters pertaining to family finances, academic progress, or student behavior. In all of these cases and more, strict adherence to guidelines of confidentiality is required to maintain trust within the board and the greater community, to preserve respectful relationships with families and school personnel, and to ensure productive results for all of the work of the board.

Confidentiality is an important aspect of creating a sense of safety in the work of the board. It contributes to a spirit of worship. Care must be taken that it is not used, wittingly or unwittingly, for purposes of over-control among a few individuals. When this happens, trust breaks down. It may be that openness is what is really needed to nourish trust in a particular situation. Sometimes trust is earned by being open, by not withholding motives, reasons, or explanations. On the other hand, sometimes trust is earned by knowing how and when to keep confidences. There is no formula for this balance. Rather, it is a constant process of discerning the right relationship between openness and confidentiality, through which a sense of mutual trust will grow (Larrabee, 2002).

In keeping with the important guidelines of the Sarbanes-Oxley legislation, Friends school boards ensure appropriate transparency by making sure they have three policies in place:
- An anti-discrimination policy
- A conflict of interest policy
- A whistle-blower policy

■ *What are best practice methods used by board clerks for leading effective meetings?*

The role of board clerk is parallel to the position of board president in other organizations, and the position of committee clerk is parallel to the role of committee chair elsewhere. Furthermore, in a Friends school the role of the board clerk involves a commitment to understanding, using, and facilitating Quaker process, as well as discerning when not to use it. The clerk is a leader whose job is not to dominate with his or her perceptions, but rather to help liberate the perceptions and truth available to those present. A good clerk will be proactive in helping the board to move to a shared decision. (See also Chapter 3.)

The clerk is a facilitator of process, a diplomat, a mediator, a listener, and a reconciler during problem solving. The job of clerk requires setting aside one's own bias and feelings that may interfere with the process of the meeting. The following is from a description of the role of clerk in Philadelphia Yearly Meeting's *Faith and Practice* (1997):

> The clerk helps the Meeting move through the agenda with efficient but unhurried dispatch, keeping the members' attention on the matters to be considered. The clerk listens, learns, and sifts, searching for the sense of the meeting, possibly suggesting tentative minutes [statements clarifying the group's understanding] or periods of silent worship to help clarify or focus Friends' leadings. The clerk encourages those who are reluctant to speak, and in like manner restrains those who tend to speak at undue length or to speak too often.

In addition to facilitating the process of board meetings, the clerk also plays a pivotal role outside of meetings, to support and guide trustees in working together for the good of the school. This support and guidance may take the form of listening or counseling, or otherwise engaging with board members to help foster more constructive collaboration for the board as a whole.

In cases where board members may be overstepping the appropriate boundaries of their roles, the clerk or the executive committee may determine a need for "eldering." In the Quaker sense of the term, eldering is the exercise of compassionate leadership, either to support and encourage a person toward an action, or to question or discourage an individual whose conduct is deemed inappropriate or harmful (see Glossary).

In Quaker meeting for worship with attention to business, the clerk of the Meeting has the following responsibilities, which may be used as a model for the job of the clerk of a Friends school board:

- Setting the tone: creating an inclusive tone, one of listening and guidance;
- Ensuring that the board meets with a prepared agenda at a given time and place;
- Starting the meeting on time, and beginning and ending the meeting with a period of worship;
- Presenting the agenda, noting which issues are for decision and which are for discussion only;
- Keeping the agenda moving, sensing when it is important to move forward or to stop and labor over a particular matter;
- Recognizing people to speak and, if appropriate, calling forward the views of those who are silent;
- Speaking the difficult truths that are not being said, the things that may be hard for others to say;

- Staying attuned to the tenor and tone of the discussion;
- Remaining a neutral facilitator, unless it is very clear that you are offering an opinion, and then considering whether someone else should be named clerk during the consideration of the particular issue;
- Fostering a climate of safety throughout all deliberations;
- Asking for a period of quiet, if a discussion seems bogged down or overly contentious;
- Encouraging reluctant speakers and reining in participants who speak too frequently or who put forward their opinions without regard to others;
- Summarizing tentative, intermediate conclusions during the process, without waiting until the end;
- Noticing when a decision is needed, then framing the issue (often with a question) and calling for discussion;
- Restating the issue as needed, summing up the "sense of the meeting" (your impression of the emerging conclusion of the group), and asking the group whether this summation is an accurate one. If so, the final decision is written as a "minute" of the meeting. If not, it will need to be revisited, immediately or at some specific point in the future;
- Helping the group figure out what action is warranted, in the event that no decision can be reached (e.g., form an ad hoc committee for further study);
- Ensuring that the group's decisions are communicated to the community, including the circulation of written minutes when appropriate;
- Performing the executive function of thinking about what needs to happen between meetings and at the next meeting, developing a sense of continuity and momentum.

In a study on leadership in Friends schools, Martha Bryans (2000) highlights three techniques used by the clerk in the Quaker process of decision making, which parallel good practice in contemporary educational leadership:

1. the formulation of a query for discussion;
2. the summary of a potential minute;
3. the call for quiet reflection during the meeting when a difficult or weighty issue is under consideration.

The applicability of these techniques highlights the synergistic space in which Friends school boards operate, namely at the confluence of sound educational leadership and good Quaker process.

What are the general responsibilities of the committees of the board and what responsibilities do specific committees have?

A strong committee structure helps to make a strong board. Clear descriptions of a committee's function and clear structures for committee responsibility, division of work, and decision making are keys to successful school governance. In a healthy and effective board, most dreaming, research, and proposal development are done or begun in committees. It is important for the board committee to seek input from various individuals and groups who may be affected by a particular decision, as well as from consultants who may have expertise on the issues. Committee-digested material is then brought to the board for its education, for discussion, and for final decision making.

Without a clear committee structure and an annual time/task chart of work for committee attention, boards may find that tasks don't get accomplished, or that board members spend too much of their time working as a whole board when committees could be more efficient. It is necessary for committees to know in advance which decisions they are responsible for making and which decisions are for the board as a whole to make. In general, the heart of committee work is to:

1. Focus questions,
2. Gather information,
3. Collect input from relevant members of the community,
4. Explore issues,
5. Craft specific action recommendations for consideration by the board as a whole.

Board membership requires that each board member be accountable for all of the board's decisions — including recommendations by committees on which one does not serve. Accordingly, it is important to note that the whole board must carefully consider committee recommendations. While a committee or task force may have given substantial effort to formulating its final proposal, the board retains its authority to approve, modify, set aside, or reject the proposal (Hammond, 2002).

Proper board protocol requires that individual trustees take full responsibility to speak their minds clearly during discussion and enter open-heartedly into the decision-making process. Then, once a decision is made, each member must support the board's decision in public — even if the decision did not go the way s/he wished. Once the decision has been made, confidentiality demands that dissenting viewpoints are not aired in public and, likewise, "who said what" is not shared. Once a decision has been made, *the board speaks as one.*

It is also important for the board as a whole to have clarity about where decision-making responsibility resides. That is, the board must know which decisions it is responsible for, and which are the responsibility of the head and others involved in the day-to-day running of the school. It is of utmost importance that board and committee members do not interfere with the day-to-day operations of the school. If a board member or board committee has questions or needs information regarding the daily operational systems, the correct route is to consult directly with the head of school. It would be inappropriate process, for example, for the clerk of the finance committee to give a task to the business manager without first consulting the head. Likewise, it would be inappropriate for a member of the personnel committee to conduct in-school observations of a faculty member who is under review. This kind of boundary crossing undermines the authority and responsibility of the head of school and gives mixed messages to the entire school community about the role and responsibility of the board and committees of the board. (See Chapter 3 for more on this topic.)

There is a great variety among Friends schools regarding the structure of board committees. Traditionally, a school board appoints regular standing committees to assist the board with its work, particularly in the areas of finance and development. The National Association of Independent Schools recommends five standing committees: Governance Committee, Resource Oversight Committee, Audit Committee, Fund Development Committee, and Executive Committee (DeKuyper, 2002). In Friends schools, given their missions, there is generally also a standing committee that oversees the Quaker dimension of school life. A brief description of the responsibilities of some of these standing committees appears below. Ad hoc committees and task forces are created when assignments can be given for specific, time-limited research and project tasks.

In addition to the committee structure proposed here, there is also a current trend for boards to reevaluate traditional committee structures. Instead of the six committees described below, a board might concentrate most of its membership in working on the top two or three strategic priorities for the school in a given year via ad hoc committees. This kind of focus might lead the board to name only a standing governance committee and a standing finance committee (for example), with other work assigned to time-delimited special task forces targeting current strategic initiatives. In this model, the roster of committees might change dramatically from year to year.

Governance Committee
This committee is named the trustees committee in some schools. If the board currently has a nominating committee, it is important to expand the scope of this committee's work to also include recruitment, orientation, training, and evaluation

of board members, as well as working for optimum quality of meetings. A common name for this committee, matching the breadth of its work as current best practice conceives it, is "governance committee." This committee is vital to the health of the board. Its members are often appointed by the clerk of the board in consultation with the executive committee. This committee is responsible for:

- Recruiting new board members who can contribute significantly to the school's strategic goals. In nominations this committee considers the ethnic, religious, racial, gender, economic, and skill diversity of the board as a whole within guidelines established by the board (and in some cases, in conjunction with the nominating committee of the Meeting).
- Ensuring that an in-depth orientation is provided for new board members
- Monitoring and taking action as needed to enhance the quality of board meetings, including planning for the development needs of individual trustees and the board as a whole
- Developing and implementing annual evaluations of the board and individual trustees
- Conducting interviews with departing trustees to learn from their experience
- Succession planning for board leadership

In the case of a school in a care relationship with a Meeting, it may be productive for the governance committee to work closely with the nominating committee from the Meeting in order to:

- Establish criteria for board members
- Assess the needs of the board in light of the school's current strategic plan/vision
- Recruit and nominate persons who meet the established criteria and the needs of the school

Executive Committee

The members of this committee generally are the clerk, the assistant clerk, the recording clerk (secretary), and the treasurer. The clerks of other standing committees may sometimes be included in an executive committee. This committee works closely with the clerk in holding the long view of the work of the board, in setting the annual board agenda for work, and in "threshing" and clarifying issues to be brought to the board. The head of school generally meets with the executive committee, and may find that this committee can bring valuable perspective to difficult issues with which the head is wrestling. This committee can play an important role as a place for the head of school and the clerk of the board to be especially candid about the joys and the frustrations of their work. The executive committee may also be given authority to act for the board in emergencies or at times when the full board is not able to gather and a decision is needed.

Finance Committee

This committee's oversight comprises the areas of finance, investments, physical assets, and property. Its work includes: overseeing the development of and adherence to the budget; reviewing the school's management of cash flow and investments; and guiding the board in considering actions that will have a financial impact on the long-term health of the school. In order to carry out all of these responsibilities, this committee may create subcommittees such as an investment subcommittee. Additionally, this committee has oversight of the health and use of school properties and buildings, including existing structures and their renewal, as well as new structures. In schools that share space with or are owned by Meetings, this committee may have joint meetings with the similar committee of the Meeting.

Audit Committee

It is a new recommendation that independent schools, including Friends schools, establish an audit committee to oversee the annual audit. It is recommended that the treasurer not serve on this committee. Some boards choose not to have any members from the finance committee serve on the audit committee, in order to assure that the board's financial oversight function can be reviewed independently by the external audit firm as part of the audit process.

Advancement Committee

This committee oversees fundraising, public relations, marketing, and institutional advancement. The responsibility for school advancement includes defining and facilitating annual development plans, supporting a busy calendar of community-building activities, overseeing internal and external relations, and creating long-range planning for raising funds needed beyond tuition revenues. Subcommittees and task forces may be created to handle large tasks.

Quaker/Spiritual Life Committee

In Friends schools, boards usually have a standing committee with special focus on the Quaker dimension of the school. This committee goes by different names in different Friends schools, such as religious life and values committee, worship and spirit committee, Quaker life committee, or spiritual life committee. In addition to board members, this committee may include the head of school, some faculty members, the head of the Quakerism or religion department, and may also include interested students, parents, and Friends meeting members.

This committee focuses on the quality of the spiritual life of the school, including meetings for worship and meetings for business and holds a special responsibility to lift up the Quaker dimension of school life for the board's awareness. Examples of methods used to nurture the spiritual life of the school include:

- Generating queries for reflection on Quaker-based practices and testimonies in the school for use by the board, as well as by the administration and faculty;
- Initiating the creation of a "Faith and Practice" document for the school community (see Friends Council website for examples from several schools);
- Designing action steps for the strategic plan that focus on maintaining and developing the Quaker ethos of the school, and prioritizing Friends testimonies (SPICES);
- Initiating special events and/or orientations related to Quaker history and practice.

The board of the Friends Council on Education and the local Friends Meeting and geographic Friends Yearly Meeting are good resources for support and guidance in this area.

Can board committees include individuals who are not trustees?

Many schools expand the power of their committees by including co-opted members in the work. Co-opted members are individuals who serve on board committees but who are not (or are not yet) board members. Co-opted members may also serve on ad hoc board committees and task forces. This method allows for adding expertise when board membership is already full. It also allows boards to train or season potential new membership. It's important to be clear when inviting co-opted members into service. Be sure to state that they're being asked to serve on a committee of the board but not the board itself and that this is a regular practice of your board. Be careful not to promise future board membership to co-opted members of committees, ad hoc committees, or task forces; leave this option open for future decision making.

Care must be taken in bringing in co-opted members to a committee, as they may not have had the same training and orientation as board members. The committee clerk, or a designated committee member, can take responsibility for orienting co-opted committee members to the spiritual underpinnings of decision making, the importance of confidentiality, and the process that the board uses for approval of committee recommendations.

In many schools, school staff report to and serve in a supportive function for specific board committees. Staff responsibilities differ from school to school, but may include active participation in planning and visioning, recording and distributing minutes (after review by committee clerk), support with clerical tasks, scheduling, and communication. Staff participation is often crucial in ensuring good communication and efficient coordination of tasks. Naturally, such staff assignments must be integrated into staff members' overall job descriptions, and must first be approved by the head.

▪ *How do we obtain the best members for highly engaged and effective committee and board functioning?*

In selecting members of the board and its constituent committees, attention must be paid to bringing ample and appropriate human resources to the board table. Even in small schools, the number of board members must be large enough to create a critical mass for the many tasks that are required for sound governance. Equally important, attention must be brought to selecting strong individuals from the many categories of expertise needed for effective board work. Care must be given to balancing overall board composition, such that members are selected who offer much-needed expertise. At the same time, the board, taken as a whole, must be able to contribute to the financial well being of the school.

Boards have a vital opportunity to get the best people on board by starting their nominating process with a system to observe and cultivate candidates over time. In so doing, the board will be sure to offer a trusteeship invitation to the right people to do the job at the right time to achieve the institution's strategic goals.

An excellent time to build committee membership is actually before new trustees come on to board service. Before a nominee is invited to become a new board member, most schools schedule an extended conversation with the nominee, in which the important topics of board service can be discussed (including current strategic initiatives, recent board and school history, and expectations for trusteeship). Schools get enhanced value out of their trustees by using this time to ask about the nominee's skills and experience and to discuss current committee openings and task force opportunities. The objective will be to make the best match between a new trustee's skills and interests and current board needs. It's also valuable, but often overlooked, to let new trustees know that they have been invited into service because of specific skills, talents, or resources that they bring, and to identify specific areas in which their input and/or leadership are particularly desired.

For maximum strategic impact, boards may want to consider a stepped process, which targets recruitment keyed to strategic objectives — first identifying the skills, capacities, and resources they need, and then cultivating individuals who can bring these skills to the board table. A sample protocol for the nominating process can be found on the Friends Council's website: Resources > Governance Tools.

How does a Friends school board prepare for thoughtful and timely leadership succession?

Both the governance committee and the executive committee have responsibility for smooth leadership succession for the board and for the head of school.

The governance committee, in addition to carrying responsibility for recruiting and orienting new trustees and providing ongoing education and evaluation for board members, has the responsibility to make certain that there is leadership planning and appropriate training for the leaders of the board and board committees. The Friends Council on Education recommends term limits as a good governance practice, as term limits support the board in knowing that its membership will be continually renewed bringing fresh perspectives and approaches to the work of the board and its committees. Designing and implementing a succession plan for the officers of the board and the committee clerks ensures a vital, knowledgeable and effective board.

The executive committee works with the head of school in determining a leadership succession plan. This may be accomplished as part of the dialogue during the head's annual evaluation. When appropriate, a frank discussion about the head's vision for her/his tenure at the school and the board's vision for leadership is valuable. Pat Bassett, president of the National Association of Independent Schools, points out that two-thirds of CEOs from Fortune 1,000 companies are hired internally, the outcome of strong succession planning and effective internal leadership training as the standard for industry. In the independent school world, potential leaders are trained and cultivated in many ways. School leaders at all levels are quick to identify, mentor, and train the next generation of school leaders and promote them to various leadership roles (task force chair, department chair, division head, and/or deanships) (Bassett, 2007). There is an ample pool of potential heads of school from the substantive leadership training programs of the Friends Council on Education and NAIS.

How can a board best orient new members?

Preparing new trustees for maximum strategic productivity is best done by creating a comprehensive orientation program that can be used with every incoming cohort. Creating, implementing, evaluating, and revising the program for use the following year is usually the job of the governance committee.

Consider including some or all of the following elements in your program:
- A formal welcome letter from the clerk of the board, including a calendar for board and committee meetings for the year ahead and a written list of expectations for trusteeship
- A mentoring program
- New trustee orientation meetings (suggested: September, mid-year, end of first year) to cover the following topics: school history and current situation; strategic planning; Quaker beliefs and practices, especially those relevant to business meetings; roles, responsibilities, and boundaries for trusteeship including a strategic focus, supporting the head, confidentiality, and accepted practice for handling difficult situations.

Many schools provide the following materials to all new trustees, assigning readings in them over time:
- From Friends Council on Education (www.friendscouncil.org):
  - *Governance Handbook for Friends Schools*
  - *Principles of Good Practice for Friends School Boards*
  - *The Care Relationship*
  - *Advices and Queries for Friends School Community Life*
  - *What Does a Friends School Have to Offer?*
  - *What do Quakers say? What do we do in Friends schools?*
- From National Association of Independent Schools (www.nais.org):
  - *Trustee Handbook*
  - *Principles of Good Practice for Boards*
- From the local Yearly Meeting:
  - *Faith and Practice*
- From the school:
  - Current strategic plan
  - Current and previous year's annual budget
  - Previous year's minutes of board meetings
  - Book of collected school policies

What can improve the flow of work from the board out to committees, and from committees back to the board?

The board clerk and the executive committee have the responsibility for maintaining an orderly flow of work between committees (standing, ad hoc, task force groups) and the board. Each committee should have a clear description of its expected function and related tasks. A strong clerk will establish an agenda for this process. Committees do their work between board meetings to accomplish tasks, conduct research, discuss information, and formulate recommendations to the whole board.

It is a good idea for the board clerk to be involved in the ongoing work of committee meetings, consulting with committee clerks on agenda development, attending selected meetings, and monitoring task completion, as necessary. In planning for board meetings, the board clerk should have a method for consulting with the head of school and committee clerks in order to arrange the best flow of the board's agenda for any particular meeting. In this way, committee reports and other materials can be sent with the upcoming meeting's agenda at least a week in advance, allowing for full efficiency at the meeting. In addition, committees that have important reports related to decision-making agenda items can be given ample time at the meeting and other agenda items can be planned accordingly.

The board clerk is responsible for preparing the agenda, generally in consultation with the head and with committee clerks. Because there may not be enough time for the board to consider all of the matters that could appropriately be decided by it, it is important to be selective about which decisions are made by the whole board, and which decisions might be delegated to committees or other decision-makers. Preparing a board agenda with decision items clearly marked is useful to any meeting where decisions will be made. It is useful for committees and other small groups to prepare issues for consideration by the whole board by framing the issues succinctly and providing appropriate information. Additionally, when appropriate, discussion can be focused further by framing decisions to be made in the form of proposals.

Using a consent agenda is an excellent way to streamline the process and make more time for meaningful discussion during board meetings. A consent agenda is a list of one or more agenda items that will, in the estimation of the clerk, probably not need discussion before they can be approved. (They may not need discussion because they've been fully digested at prior meetings, they're part of the pro-forma yearly agenda, or for other reasons.) When materials are sent out prior to a board meeting, such agenda items are listed together on the agenda under the heading "Consent Agenda." Any related material to be read prior to the meeting is, of course, included in the package as well.

At the meeting, the clerk calls for approval of the consent agenda items. If all present approve, all items are approved together and time that would otherwise be spent on repetitive or unnecessary discussion is saved. However, and very important, if any one person on the board wishes to discuss any item, it is brought off the consent agenda and put on the agenda for a future meeting, when time opens to discuss it.

At board meetings, discussion precedes decision making. Distribution of recommendations or proposals and any background information supporting these actions (ideally at least a full week prior) enhances the possible richness of discussion at the time of the meeting, and also makes the process more efficient. On a Friends school board, important decisions are often preceded by several rounds of discussions among varying levels of participants in the decision-making system, allowing for greater discernment and a fuller "seasoning" of the matter. It is the experience of most Friends schools that this deliberate discernment process yields fulfilling outcomes that are ultimately best for the school.

How can we move our board meetings toward a dynamic dialogue about substantive issues?

It's important to remember that changing the style of board meetings may be difficult or uncomfortable for some members and may take time. One trustee who led his board through this transformation had these observations:

1. The clerk must be in favor of change.
2. There must be at least three or four board members who are willing to put in the effort to effect change.
3. The proposals for changing process must not be too radical at any one time.

These suggestions may be helpful:

- Get the clerk's commitment for a specific proposal for change.
- Make use of readings, outside consultants, and conferences or workshops to see the benefits of new board structure or organization. (Check Additional Resources at the end of this manual). Share these ideas with the clerk, the head of school, and the governance committee, or perhaps with the whole board.
- First, focus on the governance committee. Create a proposal for new roles and responsibilities for this committee and its members and present it to the full board for discussion and approval.
- Charge the governance committee with the responsibility of leading the work on researching and implementing up-to-date best practices in board work. Bring all proposals to the full board for discussion and approval.
- Give the board three to five years to implement all the changes that would be advantageous. Put ideas for enhanced structure and processes on paper, and carefully test out new actions on a projected timeline.
- Change comes best when introduced incrementally, so make time for discussion and investment to occur taking time afterward for reflection.

CHAPTER 8

Creating an Optimum Culture for School Leadership and Governance

▪ *How can we create an optimum culture for school leadership and governance?*

Heads and trustees work hard to support each other in the crucial work that they perform. It can be assumed that all parties share large measures of good will and a strong desire for things to go well in school leadership. Despite the best of intentions, disagreements or clashes between ideas, principles, or people often get in the way, slowing down or undoing the hard work that's been invested by people who care passionately about their school's success. These different views can bring disagreements and conflict, and research shows that sometimes conflict can have its beneficial outcomes. But all too often, in the press of all the work that must be done, we're most saliently aware of the detriments. How can we reap the benefits available in the challenge of competing views and principles, while at the same time avoiding unnecessary losses? Research tells us that we can create that optimum culture on the board by investing in strong board development.

▪ *How can we tell if the board is strong?*

Three researchers, Chait, Holland, and Taylor (1991) looked at the boards of independent colleges to see 1) if they could correctly judge a board's strength as outsiders, and 2) if having a strong board had any impact on institutional success. While Friends schools and colleges are different in many respects, the findings of this study may have importance for governing boards of all educational institutions. What they discovered conclusively showed that strong boards are identifiable by their actions, and that it's entirely possible to improve board practice with training. They found that strong boards could be characterized by the following six dimensions of board behavior:

The Competencies of Governing Boards
(adapted from Chait et al, 1991)

I. *Contextual Dimension.* The board understands and takes into account the culture and norms of the institution that it governs. The board:
- Adapts to the distinctive characteristics and culture of the school's environment.
- Relies on the school's mission, values, and traditions as a guide for decisions.
- Acts so as to exemplify and reinforce the school's core values.

II. *Educational Dimension.* The board takes the necessary steps to ensure that trustees are well-informed about the school, the profession of education, and the board's roles, responsibilities, and performance. The board:
- Consciously creates opportunities for trustee education and development.
- Regularly seeks information and feedback on its own performance.
- Pauses periodically for self-reflection, to diagnose its strengths and limitations, and to examine its mistakes.

III. *Interpersonal Dimension.* The board nurtures the development of trustees *as a group,* attends to the board's *collective* welfare, and fosters a sense of cohesiveness. The board:
- Creates a sense of inclusiveness among trustees.
- Develops group goals and recognizes group achievements.
- Identifies and cultivates leadership within the board.

IV. *Analytical Dimension.* The board recognizes complexities and subtleties in the issues it faces and draws upon multiple perspectives to dissect complex problems and to synthesize appropriate responses. The board:
- Approaches problems from a broad institutional outlook.
- Searches widely for concrete information and actively seeks different viewpoints from multiple constituencies.
- Tolerates ambiguity and recognizes that complex matters rarely yield to perfect solutions.

V. *Political Dimension.* The board accepts as one of its primary responsibilities the need to develop and maintain healthy relationships among key constituencies. The board:
- Respects the integrity of the governance process and the legitimate roles and responsibilities of other stakeholders.
- Consults often and communicates directly with key constituencies.
- Attempts to minimize conflict and win/lose situations.

VI. *Strategic Dimension.* The board helps envision and shape institutional direction and helps ensure a strategic approach to the school's future. The board:
- Cultivates and concentrates on processes that sharpen priorities.
- Directs its attention to priorities or decisions of strategic or symbolic magnitude to the school.
- Anticipates potential problems and acts before issues become urgent.

Does board competence measurably impact school success?

The researchers compared boards with strong marks on these six competencies against a set of financial indicators published in the popular press, tracking:
- changes in total operating funds
- changes in total enrollment income
- institutional wealth and reserve funds
- proportion of institutional investment in the academic program

Interestingly, schools with strong boards did well on the financial indicators, showing an overall upward trend on the financial indicators. Conversely, schools with weak boards showed a decline in the same indicators. While it may certainly be accepted that financial strength is only one indicator of school success, there is value from reflection on these findings.

What is known about conflict at the governance level in school life?

Daily life is full of conflicts, large and small. Most of the time they don't register as problematic, but when a school finds itself involved in a serious controversy, emotions may run high and discomfort can be great. Usually, conflicts fall into one of three categories: conflicts over substance, conflicts over process, or personality conflicts (Board Source, 2008). Regardless of the source of conflict, for those holding responsibility for the long-term health and success of the school, conflict can be scary, as it may be perceived as representing a threat to enrollment, reputations, and more. For these good reasons, school leaders may choose to remain quiet about conflicts in their schools; however, this makes it difficult for individuals to learn about the sources and effects of conflict.

In order to discover information that might be useful to school leaders, a research study was conducted with heads and trustees of Friends schools under the auspices of the Friends Council on Education (Christensen, 2005). Six findings from the study may be of particular interest to school leaders:

1. Over 93 percent of respondents to the study's survey reported that they'd experienced significant conflict (self-defined) at the board level, showing that conflict is indeed a common experience.

2. The head, the board as a whole, and parents were named more often than any other group or individual as involved in conflict, with the head named 30 percent more often than the board, and 50 percent more often than parents. (This information may not come as a surprise when we consider that the head has the authority for all operational decisions and that the head is, by role, at the center of the wheel of contact in the school community.)

3. Some boards had prepared themselves well for governance (by engaging in processes for strategic nominations, orientation of new members, ongoing professional development of trustees, and giving attention to best practices for discussion and decision making). These boards reported experiencing a) less conflict, b) less distress in the context of conflict, and c) reduced institutional or interpersonal damage as the result of conflict.

4. Even well-prepared boards often reported the presence of some distress during conflict — indicating that, while perhaps inevitable, conflict may never be entirely comfortable.

5. Several practices were seen to be productive in dealing positively with conflict when it did occur:
   - Developing a culture of direct communication
   - Using outside experts or peers from other schools for consultation
   - Making good use of Quaker processes for discussion and discernment

6. Some schools reported making important gains in the aftermath of conflict — in the form of interpersonal and/or institutional growth. One, single factor correlated with experiencing growth: establishing a culture of curiosity on the board.

What are the takeaway lessons from this research?

- By making the time to build a strong board culture and by anticipating and preparing for potential problems, many difficulties can be minimized or avoided.
- It can be predicted that conflicts will occur often and that the head and the board will likely be involved in them. By working together, using well-developed and trusted processes, board and head can move through these times successfully.
- Best of all, personal and institutional growth can be maximized by taking steps to build a culture of curiosity on the board and in the school.

■ *What processes do Friends schools use to work with conflict in school life?*

An important discrimination that a board can make for a Friends school community is to articulate the difference between several perceived "Quaker" processes that can be used to resolve conflicts or to air a complaint. The following descriptions may be useful. Note that these processes are most useful when all participants enter into discussion with open minds and a willingness to listen to others.

Conflict resolution: The goal of a conflict resolution process is for persons involved in a conflict to work together to clarify facts and feelings and to come to a resolution of the conflict. Most Friends schools emphasize conflict resolution in their work with students, and many schools have developed their own conflict resolution manuals. (See www.friendscouncil.org for resources.) Many Friends schools train older students to be peer mediators in the conflict resolution process with other students. The Friends School in Minnesota has developed a well-known conflict resolution program, which provides training, consultation and ongoing support for faculty and students in independent and public schools. What is missing in many schools is a detailed conflict resolution process for adults. It would be valuable for schools that have well-developed conflict resolution procedures for their students to adapt these procedures in developing a standard conflict resolution process for adults in the community (faculty, staff, parents, head, board).

Clearness process: Clearness, as a Quaker process, is commonly described in general terms in Friends Yearly meeting *Faith and Practice* documents. The Friends Council on Education has developed a number of clearness protocols for use in schools and meetings, available at www.friendscouncil.org. The goal of a clearness process is different from mediation, conflict resolution, or group decision making. A clearness process is used when a person wants to reflect deeply on an issue, concern, or decision to be made and would like to do this with the support of a small group of people who can listen in worshipful atmosphere, holding the focus person in the Light. The group members in a clearness process do not give advice, make judgments, or recommend outcomes. They listen deeply and may provide "clearness quality" questions that will support the focus person in reflecting more deeply and listening to her/his own inner teacher, Inner Light. The goal of a clearness process is to support a person in reaching a deeper understanding of the issue and clarity about how to move forward. The underlying assumptions of the clearness process are:

- Each of us has an Inner Light that can guide us; therefore, the answers sought are within the person seeking clearness.
- The clearness process embodies the paradox of solitude and community. It is grounded in the belief that there are no external authorities on life's deepest issues. There is only the authority (the Light) that lies within each of us waiting to be heard.
- A group of caring friends/colleagues can serve as channels for spirit-led guidance in drawing out the inner teacher.

Grievance: It is useful to note that "grievance" procedures were created by labor unions and the term "grievance" implies a legal process with the goal of a legal resolution to a conflict. A grievance procedure often involves bringing in a trained legal mediator. Since the majority of Friends schools are not unionized, most Friends schools do not have documented grievance procedures.

Meeting for Listening: When there is disagreement in the faculty, parent, or board community, or discontent arises, as it normally may over time, the board and head, together, may agree to use a specific process with the goal that community members may feel heard. A key element here is to find a way to plan together, head and board, for that information gathering. In the instance where a number of people have a common complaint, when a complaint has been raised and seems to persist, despite best efforts to resolve it, some heads and boards decide together to plan a "meeting for listening" or to appoint a "listening committee."

First, board or board and head decide who will be invited to speak and who will listen. The head may attend or not. If the head and board together decide the head will not attend, they also decide if all information will be shared or if the sharing will be kept to summary points, keeping names and specific comments confidential (knowing that there are advantages to either method).

In this format, individuals are invited to share their perspective in a frank and honest way. It's imperative that speakers do not get the impression that this will be a court of appeals, a way of over-riding a decision made by the head. The purpose of the meeting for listening is that all know the board has heard them. The clerk may reflect back summarized or reframed content, to let the speaker know s/he has been heard. Speakers are thanked and are told that the board will take their information under consideration. Information gathered is organized and shared with the head, if the head was not present. Finally, the board and head together engage in using the information for future action (or not).

Threshing Session: This is a planned gathering to consider a controversial issue in a way that is free from the necessity of reaching any decision. A well-managed threshing session can be valuable for getting all of the information and perspectives related to an issue in the open, so that the views and information can be used for future deliberations and decision making by the appropriate group or person.

How does the board know how the head is doing?

How does the board know, for sure, how the head is doing? How can board members maintain public support of the head without actually seeing what the head does day to day?

The most vital question is how does the board maintain a proper openness to information regarding the performance of the head, which is needed for a realistic appraisal, without opening itself to complaints? The keys are to:

1. Build and carefully maintain a close, frank, and mutual relationship of trust with the head;

2. Together with the head, plan for gathering the information that is needed to assess the performance of the head. For the head to trust the board in this, s/he needs to know that any information heard by a trustee will be shared openly with the head, that no secrets will be held, that all parties will follow the "no surprises" rule. While it may be initially uncomfortable to share a negative comment with the head, it could eventually turn out to be more destructive for a trustee or a board to hold those comments in confidence, as this could undermine the trust between the head and board.

Valuable information can be gained in the course of an annual review of the head's performance. Many boards designate this task to the executive committee or an ad-hoc head evaluation committee. Various forms of evaluation are used, including:

- a review of the head's written goals for the year, compared with the year's progress;
- a short survey of the board assessing the head's performance on the major goals for the year and the major dimensions of the head's role and responsibilities;
- a survey of a small number of representative individuals from various school constituencies;
- a full 360 degree process, involving a larger number of individuals;

- a portfolio process
- a broad school satisfaction survey that includes a few items related to the role of the head.

As with other forms of evaluation, it's best to change methods from time to time. That way, curiosity may be maximized, opening space for fresh perspectives. (See the group for Friends School Board Clerks at www.friendscouncil.net, for examples of evaluation forms and processes.)

What does the board do with information gathered? Normally a small committee of the board, which includes the board clerk, works with the head to use the information gathered in the context of professional development, so that the head can set goals and action steps based on the feedback. In the evaluation process, it is important that the board not use negative feedback to publicly over-rule a decision of the head or undermine the credibility of the head. The board can properly, however, pass this information on to the head and, if there is a close and trusting relationship already established, the head may solicit input from the board in moving into the future with the situation. It is very important that the board maintain seamless public support of the head while any disagreements between the board and the head are aired between them confidentially, and in private. (The notable exception to this rule is if, in the process of gathering feedback, the board decides the head has done something illegal. In that case, the prudent course of action is to consult with a trusted lawyer and proceed according to the lawyer's recommendations.)

Just as the board has important work to do to earn and keep the trust of the head, it is vital that the head communicate openly with the board, keeping the board (not just the board clerk) apprised of serious complaints or discontent from within the school community if and when these arise. Trust is built by handling these issues openly and directly between the head and the board.

In sum, the overall goal for long-term success is to create a close, trusting, partnership of equals between the board and the head.

What are respectful and supportive methods for learning about the head's performance and working on issues that may arise?

Trust is built daily from tested expectations, and trust building is fundamental to a well-functioning community. Stephen M.R. Covey (2006), a leading organizational consultant, contends that the best way to build the output of your organization and to experience more high-quality work accomplished in less time, thereby reducing costs — is to build trust. With that thought in mind, here are some processes that, used correctly, can gather valuable information about the head's performance while building trust and increasing the flow of important and reliable information throughout your community.

Head's Reports

One important feature of the regular reports to their boards that heads may make is an update on school climate, including even a brief review of criticisms that may be coming to the attention of the head and how s/he is handling them. Developing comfort with discussing difficulties and problem-solving around them will go a long way in building board capacity to understand larger complaints when they occur (as they're likely to), as well as to withstand accompanying discomfort, without losing perspective. The best boards, especially when considering difficult decisions, budget time to anticipate potential conflict before it occurs — building analytic capacity, resilience, and general "board emotional intelligence."

Regular Meetings between Head and Board Clerk

One of the best ways to avoid difficulties and build for strength is to schedule regular meetings, at which both parties can share current news and prioritize goals, before any urgency is felt. Creating additional time to support a new or inexperienced head will be more than made up for in greatly increased progress toward strategic goals and reduced time needed to address mistakes that may otherwise occur.

360 Degree Evaluation Process

A 360 degree process for gathering feedback information about the head's performance can be periodically useful in schools. Generally, the board clerk or clerk of the governance/trustee/nominating committee works with the head to construct a list of questions and a list of community members who will be contacted (ranging from a representative sample to all members of the community). Often, an online survey tool is used to solicit and compile the feedback. The board clerk or a small committee may summarize the feedback for discussion with the head.

■ *What is an "executive session" of the board and when is it appropriate to hold an executive session?*

An executive session of the board includes all full board members and very often includes the head of school. Ex-officio members of the board, such as staff, faculty representatives, and parent representatives, do not attend an executive session. Executive sessions may be held periodically when a confidential matter (the annual budget, for example) needs to be brought to the board by the head or by the clerk of the finance committee, when the board engages in its annual self-evaluation, or for evaluation of the head of school. (The head's evaluation is an example of one of the times when the head might not attend.)

It is recommended that boards build into their regular functioning periodic opportunities to convene without the presence of the head, and with the full knowledge and support of the head. Doing this actually builds trust, rather than undermining it, because all parties understand that the dynamic health of the system depends upon the board and the head having their own "space" to thresh, discern and deliberate, without anyone perceiving such activity to be a threat to the other partner. Building this protocol will support healthy "checks and balances" needed in good school governance.

Executive sessions are often scheduled, for convenience, prior to or immediately following a regularly scheduled board meeting. When an executive session of the board is held, it uses the same spirit-led Quaker process as a regular board meeting. The clerk leads the meeting and the recording clerk writes clear minutes of any decisions (though s/he does not record the discussion).

In order to build trust between the board and the head, when an executive session is held without the head, it's imperative that the head be notified of this session and its purpose in advance of the meeting, and that the board clerk inform the head at least in general terms about the content of the discussion afterward, having let the board know that s/he will be doing so (Board Source, 2008). Scheduling regular, periodic, or occasional (when necessary) executive sessions without the head allows for time when both formal evaluations and informal information sharing regarding the head's performance may be planned and performed by the board in a professional, organized, and properly-channeled manner.

▪ *What if members of the community voice critical complaints about the head directly to members of the board?*

An experienced trustee and former head of school observed, "When a school hires a new head, everyone is looking for Superman or Superwoman. The trouble is, sooner or later they always realize the new head is just human." And when that realization occurs, whether in the first year or later, the wise board will be ready to properly field critical comments and complaints, supporting the head and sharing information with the head.

The two main jobs of the board are:
1. to hire, support, evaluate, and (if necessary) dismiss the head;
2. to ensure the long-term health and sustainability of the school.

Experienced trustees know that successfully accomplishing the first task is a complex and delicate job, and that doing it well goes a long way in advancing the second job of the board. An important support is encouraging the head in her/his ongoing professional development (time for networking and developing crucial peer relationships with other local heads, having a dedicated budget line for the head's ongoing education). Wise boards are very careful not to overstep into the domain of the head by interfering in the daily operations of school life. Successful boards make time for trustee training specifically on appropriate interaction with a complaining parent, teacher, or Friends Meeting member. This training includes examples of how to clearly and politely direct the person with a complaint to speak with the person who can do something about the complaint, which in most cases would be a teacher (for a parent) or the head (for a faculty member or Friends Meeting member). We might call this the "direct talk protocol."

The board that has a clear view of its role will see the occasional complaint as a teachable moment for the community, a time when roles and related responsibilities, as well as important communication channels and confidentiality boundaries can be articulated for learning. Of course, it takes many such moments to teach a whole community and if all trustees are not on the same page, if some trustees make the mistake of engaging (and therefore encouraging) complaints, the work will be harder. Some proven ways to get all trustees on board with the direct talk protocol are:

- Build this training into the new trustee orientation.
- Plan a short educational time to discuss the issue in a board meeting every year.
- Make time for role play practice so that strategic responses and behaviors can be called up more easily when they're needed in challenging situations.
- Anticipate controversies and plan effective trustee responses to them before they arise.

It's a fine line, not getting too involved; any experienced trustee knows that complaints will come their way. However, diligent trustees do not allow themselves to become complaint departments, second-guessing or countermanding the decisions of the head. To do this is to risk undermining the authority of the head in a grievous way. Yet, trustees cannot entirely close themselves off from feedback from the school community, either — at the risk of failing in the board's duty to stay aware of the performance of its only employee. Establishing proper and mutually agreed-upon channels of communication is essential to avoiding a buildup of frustration or pressure within the school community, and the likely accompanying rumor mill, which can arise if there are difficulties and community members do not feel heard.

When persistent patterns of feedback are given to multiple trustees about the head's leadership, this is a time for the board clerk to think out loud with the head about how to best manage negative perceptions. While trustees should not encourage gossip and complaining, they must also remain astute to patterns they may witness in their roles, which contribute to a lack of confidence about the school and its leadership. When patterns emerge from negative feedback, the board can work with the head to create a process by which the issues are resolved.

During a time of difficulty it is important to maintain trust and openness between the head and the board, sharing information as it is learned and planning next steps together. As this period may be especially stressful for the head, it is a good time for the board to ask what it can do concretely to support the head. And, while board and head are working hard to resolve problems, the board must work purposefully to maintain the confidence and energy of the head, a precious and not-easily-renewable resource for the school.

When the termination of a head's contract must be considered, it is critical to do so in a thoughtful, respectful way. An abrupt termination of contract may result in: loss of trust and loss of effective leadership for the remainder of the time head and board work together; potential loss of families, trustees, staff, or donors; a reduced ability to attract a skilled and informed candidate to be the next head; and, a setback in the community's ability to build a culture of direct communication. Precipitous action can be avoided by sharing information and solving problems together throughout the course of a head's tenure — to be the benefit of all parties: board, head, and especially the school.

■ *What attitudes and tools are helpful in the heat of discussion?*

It is human nature for difficult feelings to arise around challenging issues, particularly when discussion becomes heated. One excellent way to reduce tension and anxiety at these times is to build a long-term board culture of inquiry. To increase the chances of surfacing novel solutions to difficult questions an optimum board culture is promoted with an attitude of *staying curious*. This can be a board goal for the year and a goal for individual committees. It can be handled as simply as designating a board member to be the "curiosity reminder," someone who will at important times interject a question like: *How can we maintain curiosity in the upcoming discussion?*

Boards may find good use in time-honored Quaker practices, such as:
- Taking time to settle into silence before (or during) challenging discussion,
- Reviewing the attitude to bring to Quaker-based decision making (see Chapter 3),
- Beginning with a focusing query to shed light on the current discussion,
- Holding a threshing session.

Schools use a variety of helpful exercises as board development opportunities or to add useful structure in the moment, when they must move through a difficult discussion. See www.friendscouncil.org for a selection of these exercises, including:
- The Cone in the Box
- The Jigsaw Puzzle
- The Hidden Hinge
- The Rule of Six

CHAPTER 9

Relationships Across the School Community

Why is it important for the board to nurture good relationships in a Friends school?

A major satisfaction for many Friends school board members is the experience of *work intimacy*. Work intimacy grows from a shared sense of higher purpose, a deep intellectual meeting of the minds, and the courageous dialogue required for moral leadership, especially in difficult times. Accordingly, cultivating good interpersonal relationships is a primary responsibility of individual board members and the corporate body of the board in a Friends school.

It is in the relationships between people that the ethos of a good Friends school is immediately recognizable. The ethos is visible through the careful, respectful good will that occurs in the contact between the many groups and individuals who make up the school family: the faculty, the parents, the students, the staff, the administration, the alumni/ae, the Meeting, and the board. The responsibility of creating and fostering an atmosphere — a culture — in which all these groups, and the individuals within them, feel themselves to be valued rests ultimately with the expectations set by the board. More than any other single factor, this warmth, mutual trust, and sense of the worth of oneself and others make up that quality that distinguishes a religiously-motivated school. In fact, this is the soil that makes the experience of a spirit-led school possible (Committee on Education, 1986).

▪ *How can board members, individually and collectively, nurture good relationships with each of the constituencies in the school community?*

The Board and the Friends Meeting

In a Friends school, one of the board's most important responsibilities is to support and nurture the spiritual and ethical life of all those directly connected with the school, in service to the school's mission. In the case of those schools in care relationships with Friends Meetings, it is the board's responsibility to nurture relationships between the school and the Meeting, and to encourage the head to take initiative in this area, as well. It is likewise important for the Meeting to be concerned for the spiritual life of the school. The board may encourage Friends Meeting members to share in the meetings for worship held by the school, and in like manner, the Meeting may reach out to invite parents and faculty to attend meeting for worship on Sunday. Often a school board arranges a special September meeting for worship at the meetinghouse for parents and faculty new to the school. Sensitive understanding of the needs and the strengths of the Meeting and the school should flow back and forth through the board.

The board serves as a communication channel between the Friends Meeting and the school. Many boards create a Quaker life committee to focus on maintaining and nourishing the dynamic relationship between the school and the Meeting, and to support the Quaker ethos of the school. This committee usually comprises board members and Meeting members, and may include the head of school or interested faculty and students.

In the case of a school in a care relationship with a Friends Meeting, it is crucial that the board take a leadership role in discerning and clarifying the mutual expectations and parameters of the school-Meeting relationship. In this context, it is necessary to acknowledge the different constituencies and different purposes that the school and the Meeting serve. Given this, it is essential that both groups work to regularly cross the divides of their separate realities. Through recognizing the possibility for misunderstanding and conflict that differences may bring, the board can lead the school and the Meeting in creating systematic processes for productive communication, information sharing, and relationship-building (Seaver, 2002). (Friends Council on Education and local Quaker resources can provide helpful consultation for this process, along with examples of practice from other school-Meeting relationships. See also chapter 1 of this handbook regarding "care relationships.")

In those schools in which the board is a committee of the Friends Meeting, and therefore in a care relationship with the Meeting, it is important that roles and responsibilities between the board and the Meeting are mutually clear and understood.

This clarity and mutuality will go a long way toward addressing potential conflicts of interest, as well as toward helping individuals to differentiate between their own roles as Meeting member and school trustee. While overlapping and mutually supportive, this dual identity can place people in awkward — and potentially compromising — situations. Similarly, clarity about roles and responsibilities in the school-Meeting relationship builds a reservoir of mutual trust and good feelings, which can be drawn upon when there is a major decision to be made that is likely to affect both the school and the Meeting communities.

It is noteworthy in this context that in recent years numerous Meeting-school pairs have chosen the route of separate incorporation, each becoming a separate legal entity, with its own articles of incorporation and by-laws. In cases where this step has been taken, both parties have recognized that this new relationship format provides an appropriate legal mechanism for the right stewardship of both institutions (Meeting and school), while safeguarding and emphasizing their joint commitment to the Quaker dimension of the school's mission. This includes schools in care relationships with Yearly Meetings as well as schools in care relationships with Monthly and Quarterly Meetings. In such cases, the by-laws may be written to describe how the nominating committee of the Meeting may continue to work in coordination with the board's governance committee to define board member qualifications and develop a process for the appointment of board members.

The Board, the Faculty, Administration and Support Staff

The head, often in consultation with a search committee and/or input from faculty colleagues, hires teachers and staff. The board's role with faculty members is a friendly, supportive one, not supervisory. The head is responsible for supervising and evaluating the faculty and staff.

The board has an obligation to make members of the faculty feel appreciated and accepted as individuals and as professionals. Boards in Friends schools extend their good will in many simple ways, ranging from inviting individual faculty members to make program presentations at the beginning of board meetings, to inviting parents to organize a faculty appreciation luncheon. Creating a healthy, viable salary and benefits package for faculty and staff is a primary responsibility of the board. Providing ample funding for professional development activities and resources demonstrates board support for faculty and develops a strong faculty for the school. It is a great benefit to the community when the board and the faculty are aware of each others' work.

It is *not* recommended for schools to have faculty members serve in a board role. If done, this must be handled with great care due to the inherent conflict of interest in the faculty member's role. It is undeniable that faculty are the beating heart of school life; however, first and foremost, faculty are charged with seeing to the best interests of current students — while the board's primary charge is to the health and sustainability of the school for future generations. Confounding these two roles (faculty member as board member) creates a conflict of interest apparent in matters of budget, finance, and personnel policy, especially considering that a faculty member on the board would act in the role of the "boss" of the head — who is, by definition, the faculty member's boss. If a board does include a faculty member, it's better to make the role a faculty representative rather than full board member. Individuals selected must be carefully trained in taking off the "faculty hat" and taking on a holistic, long-range view. Additionally, specific provision must be made for going into executive session without faculty with guidelines for doing so made clear to all before faculty are brought on to board service.

The Board and Parents

The board is responsible to encourage the development of a strong parent organization. While a Friends school board often includes in its membership some parents of current students, parents who serve as board members must remove their "parent hat" at board meetings. By temporarily setting aside the parent role, a board member can participate in decision making about the overall health of the school most faithfully and effectively. While boards may try to limit the number of current parents on their membership roster, many find that alumni/ae parents make extremely effective trustees. No longer pressed by the short-term issues that may unduly sway current parents, parents of alumni/ae know the school well, deeply appreciate its values, and may be exceedingly strong advocates for its long-term success.

The Board and Alumni/ae

The board is urged to be mindful that its mission of outreach to students and their families does not cease when the students graduate. A strategic board considers enthusiastic and capable alumni/ae for board membership and works with alumni/ae in development and fundraising to ensure the school's stable and healthy future.

The Board and the Larger Community

In support of its role as champion of the school's mission, the board is under the weight of promoting the institutional success of the school through its relationships with all constituencies in the larger community. It is the responsibility of each board member to consider the ways in which her or his own network of relationships might have a beneficial impact upon the life of the school. Enormous benefits are realized through the simple cultivation of good will, and through the generous sharing of positive school experiences in the external community. In the long-term view, positive relations with the surrounding community will strengthen the school as well as the community.

Given the crucial importance of supporting and nurturing the head of school, are there specific things that the board is encouraged to do in this regard?

A good relationship between the board and the head of school is fundamental to the lively, healthful functioning of the school. In Friends schools, as in other independent schools, the board is primarily responsible for policy-making, for financial planning and strategic planning, and for hiring and nurturing the head. The head is responsible for managing all aspects of day-to-day operation of the school, for hiring and evaluating personnel, implementing board policy, overseeing curriculum, as well as visioning with the board. (See responsibility charting for decision making in Chapter 3.)

In those cases where the board and head mutually understand and respect each others' roles and responsibilities, the synergy may be taken for granted, because the collaboration feels so "natural" and good. By contrast, however, the absence of such mutuality may deplete the energies and good will of the head as well as the board members, to the detriment of the whole community. Like all human relationships, the board-head relationship requires commitment and ongoing effort by all parties.

The board is responsible for:
- supporting the professional development of the head (including providing funds for this purpose),
- making sure that the head's job responsibilities are manageable without burnout,
- providing a clear process of annual goal-setting and evaluation for the head.

It is vital for the board to establish clear areas of responsibility for the head, and for the board and head to collaborate on providing concrete ways for board members, individually and collectively, to demonstrate their support for the head. In the case of a new head of school, it is particularly critical during the initial years of her or his tenure that the board provide extra levels of support and nurturance, as the new head learns about the culture and management of the school. The nature and scope of such extra support will depend upon the school culture, the personalities, and the dynamic context at the time of the new head's arrival.

In a Friends school, the board has the special responsibility of charging the head with operating the school on the foundation of the principles and practices of the Religious Society of Friends as well as the principles of good practice of the Friends Council on Education and the National Association of Independent Schools. Sometimes this requires that the board engage in a continuing-education process about Friends education and

Quaker-based decision making, perhaps engaging the services of a consultant. For a head that comes without a background in Friends education or Quakerism, the board is responsible to support the head in learning about Quakerism. Alternately, it may be the head who needs to challenge the board to take more leadership in caring for the Quaker ethos of the school. The Friends Council on Education provides excellent resources in this area.

Given the special importance of the partnership between the clerk of the board and the head of school, what can be done to support and nurture this relationship?

The importance of the person-to-person relationship between the clerk of the board and the head of the school can hardly be overstated. Many heads look to a clerk to be a "critical friend," i.e., both critical and friendly. Some heads view the clerk as one of the few people in the school with whom she/he is able to develop a friendship. This, of course, can be rewarding for both parties, as well as for the school. It also can be problematic, as both parties must of course retain their differential roles, and so must be approached with care. Accordingly, below are some examples of practice in support of a constructive and healthy relationship between clerk and head:

EXAMPLE 1
One head of school enumerated her expectations of the board clerk, and shared them in an appropriate way:

- Conduct interesting and meaningful board meetings with manageable time boundaries.
- Ensure that board business has a sense of continuity and focuses on long term strength of school, the next generation.
- Organize a planned agenda for board meetings and cancel meetings when there are no pressing agenda items. Be sure that agenda items have been pre-processed by committee.
- Be sure that both the head and the board clerk review the meeting minutes prior to distribution.
- Keep the board focused on policy and the head focused on operations. For example, the board may not create a program on spelling or world history or Quakerism. Nor should it define procedures for homework, report cards, sports, dress code, or rules for the school bus. If a board member thinks the school is wrong in one of these areas, refer the board member to talk with the head of school, rather than make an issue at a board meeting without knowing history, facts, and perspectives. The board clerk can request that the head prepare a report to the board, as necessary.

> **EXAMPLE 2**
>
> *In one school, the board clerk and the head of school developed a list of mutual expectations:*
>
> - Identify issues for the school, the future, and the board and flag them for consideration and possible action.
> - Develop and maintain a partnership in doing the work of leading, improving, guiding, and using the board well.
> - Keep each other informed of crises and major decisions that will have significant impact before the fact. We will not be surprised by anything each other says in a board meeting or other public setting.
> - Be honest and forthcoming in our work, behavior and communications with each other.
> - Keep appropriate communications and information in confidence.
> - Call or see each other on a weekly basis, at a specified time, whether or not there is pressing business.

The clerk-head partnership and the board-head relationship hinge on open communication and discipline enacted from a ground of faith and trust. It is important to state that there is danger in a clerk-head relationship that is too distant, losing the opportunity to vet information before action is required; just so, there is danger in a clerk-head relationship that is so strong that it takes on the quality of an exclusionary dyad. While the clerk may be the first confidante of a head, important information may not be kept from the board as a whole. Successful clerks will remember that the board speaks with one voice — not with the sole voice of the clerk. It's the job of the head, clerk, and board to make sure that all are fully informed (within requirements for confidentiality) and invested, for the long-term health and success of the school.

Perhaps no other relationship in the school depends more — or profits more — by what Covey calls "the speed of trust" in his book of that same name (2006). Making the time to build a healthy, mutually supportive relationship between the head and the clerk is worth its weight in gold when difficult decisions or school crises arise.

In sum, the long-term health of a Friends school rides on the strength of the relationships that have been cultivated across its community. More important than anything else it can do, the board must actively build trust, curiosity, and organization for strategic forward motion. With these in hand, a board can reasonably hope to look ahead many generations to a thriving and sustainable future.

References

Agazarian, Yvonne, and Susan Gantt (2000). *Autobiography of a Theory.* London: Jessica Kingsley Publishers.

Bassett Blog (2007), www.nais.org, accessed September 14, 2009.

Bassett, Patrick (Summer 2002). "Rethinking Independent School Governance," *Independent School*. National Association for Independent Schools.

Board Source (2008). *Critical Components of Effective Governance: A Practitioner Program.* Washington, D.C.

Bryans, Martha (2000). *Leadership in Friends Schools,* doctoral dissertation. Philadelphia: University of Pennsylvania.

Calder, Fred (February 2000). "Head to Head: Mutual Obligations of Head and Board Chair," Bulletin #245. New York State Association of Independent Schools.

Caldwell, Barbara Rose (1998). "The Quaker Decision-Making Process: What is it? How can we use it in a Friends School?" pamphlet. Philadelphia: Friends Council on Education.

Cary, Stephen G. (1996). "Quaker Education and Friends School Haverford," lecture. Haverford Friends Meeting, Haverford, Pa.

Carver, J., & Carver, M. M. (1997). *Reinventing Your Board: A Step-by-Step Guide to Implementing Policy Governance.* San Francisco: Jossey-Bass.

Center for Applied Research (1997). "Responsibility Charting." Philadelphia.

Chait, R., Holland, T. P., & Taylor, B. E. (1991). *The Effective Board of Trustees*. New York: Macmillan.

Christensen, Ginny (2005). *Discovering the Potential for Growth: Conflict at the Governance Level in Friends Schools,* doctoral dissertation. Santa Barbara, Ca.: Fielding Graduate Institute.

Committee on Education (1986). *Handbook for Committee Members of Friends Schools*. Philadelphia: Philadelphia Yearly Meeting.

Covey, Stephen M.R. (2006). *The Speed of Trust: The One Thing that Changes Everything.* New York: Simon and Schuster.

DeKuyper, Mary Hundley (2002). Personal communication.

DeKuyper, Mary Hundley (1998). *Trustee Handbook: A Guide to Effective Governance for Independent School Boards,* 7th edition. Washington, D.C.: National Association of Independent Schools.

DiMicco, Charlene (2002). Personal communication.

Edstene, Kay (1996). Materials for Trustees and Heads Conference. Philadelphia: Friends Council on Education.

Faith and Practice (1997). Philadelphia: Philadelphia Yearly Meeting.

Grundy, Marty Paxson. (September, 2002). "Authority," *Friends Journal.*

Hammond, J. Harry (2002, 2009). Personal communication.

Hoerle, Heather (2009). Personal communication.

Lacey, Paul (1998). *Growing into Goodness: Essays on Quaker Education.* Philadelphia: Pendle Hill and Friends Council on Education.

Larrabee, Arthur (August 18, 2002). Personal communication.

Mueller, Robert W. (2001). "Long-Range Planning as a Finance Tool," lecture. Trustees and Heads Conference, Friends Council on Education.

Ravdin, William (April 5, 2002). Personal communication.

Seaver, JoAnn (July, 2002). "A Big Event in a Small Meeting with a Small School 'Under its Care,'" *Friends Journal.*

Senge, Peter, Art Kleiner, Charlotte Roberts, Richard B. Ross, and Bryan J. Smith (1994). *The Fifth Discipline Fieldbook: Strategies and Tools for Building a Learning Organization.* New York: Doubleday.

Van Arkel, Nancy (2006). Essay for Institute for Engaging Leadership in Friends Schools, Friends Council on Education.

Glossary

Adapted from Glossary of *Faith & Practice* of Philadelphia Yearly Meeting (1997)

Note: Some of the following terms are in common usage, but Friends have given them a particular meaning. Others are essentially limited to Quaker usage.

Breaking Meeting: The act of bringing a meeting for worship to a close by shaking hands. Usually, an individual has been designated to initiate this process.

Care Relationship: A Friends school may be considered to be in a care relationship with the Meeting that sponsored its founding, and that continues to feel responsible for its spiritual and/or fiduciary well being. This term is used for a variety of configurations of responsibilities, roles, and relationships between Friends schools and meetings.

Centering/Centering Down: The initial stage of worship in which Friends clear their minds and settle down to achieve a spiritual focus.

Clearness: Confidence that an action is consistent with divine will.

Clerk: The person responsible for the administration of a Friends body and sensitive to the guidance of the Spirit in the conduct of the business of that body. This includes preparation, leadership, and follow up of meetings for business.

Concern: A quickening sense of the need to do something about a situation or issue in response to what is felt to be a direct intimation of God's will.

Continuing Revelation: A central Quaker belief that spiritual truth is revealed to us continually, in an ongoing and communal process.

Discernment: An individual and/or group process by which clarity of purpose or understanding is achieved, proceeding from a spiritual awareness or realization. Discernment is not a form of decision making, per se, but rather a precursor to decision making that rests upon a willingness to patiently listen for divine leading, in oneself and in others.

Eldering: The exercise of compassionate leadership, either to support and encourage a person toward an action, or to question or discourage an individual whose conduct is deemed inappropriate or harmful. (Formerly "Elder" was used as a term to describe an individual recognized as having significant spiritual gifts and expected to exercise special oversight of the spiritual life of the Meeting and its members.)

Experiential Religion: A religion in which personal spiritual experience is the foundation for belief and practice. The word experimental was used by early Friends with this meaning.

Gathered Meeting: A meeting for worship or for business in which those present feel deeply united in divine presence.

Good Order: Those procedures for the conduct of Friends business and witness that encourage a Meeting to carry out its corporate activities under divine leading. The term rightly ordered is also used in this sense.

Hold (a person) in the Light: To desire that divine guidance and healing will be present to an individual who is in distress or faces a difficult situation; also, to give prayerful consideration to an idea.

Integrity: One of the basic practical principles or testimonies of Friends. It involves both a wholeness and harmony of the various aspects of one's life, and truthfulness in whatever one says and does. Friends commonly link this principle with the testimony of simplicity.

Laying Down: A decision to discontinue a committee when its work is complete; occasionally, a decision to discontinue a Meeting or other Friends organization when it is no longer viable.

Laying Over: To postpone the discussion of an issue or the presentation of a report from one meeting for business to another.

Leading: A sense of being called by God to undertake a specific course of action. A leading often arises from a concern.

Lift Up: To emphasize or make explicit a particular point or concern.

Light/Inner Light: Terms that represent for Friends the direct, unmediated experience of the divine. Some other equivalent terms often found in Quaker writings are: the spirit, the spirit of Truth, the divine principle, the seed, the guide, the inward teacher, that of God in every person.

Meeting for Worship: A gathering of individuals in quiet waiting upon the enlightening and empowering presence of the divine; the central focus of the corporate life of the Religious Society of Friends.

Meeting for Worship for Business: A meeting for worship during which the corporate business of the Meeting is conducted — often referred to as meeting for business.

Mind the Light: An admonition to attend to the Light within for guidance in one's life. It means both active obedience to divine leadings and careful nurturing of one's openness to the Light.

Minute: The record of a corporate decision reached during a meeting for worship for business. More broadly, the account of a single transaction in the written record of a meeting for business or other body.

Monthly Meeting: 1) A congregation of Friends who meet regularly for worship and to conduct corporate business. 2) A monthly gathering of such a body for worship and business.

Opening: A term often used by early Friends to designate a spiritual opportunity or leading.

Peace Testimony: The corporate commitment of Friends to pacifism and nonviolence.

Proceed As Way Opens: To undertake a service or course of action without prior clarity about all the details but with confidence that divine guidance will make these apparent and assure an appropriate outcome.

Programmed Meeting: A Friends Meeting under the leadership of a pastor, with an arranged order of worship that usually includes a period of silent worship. [cf., Unprogrammed Meeting].

Quaker: Originally, a derogatory term applied to Friends because their excitement of spirit when led to speak in a meeting for worship was sometimes expressed in a shaking or quaking motion. Now this term is simply an alternative designation for a member of the Religious Society of Friends.

Quaker Process: A catch-all expression often used to describe the various and collective techniques by which Quakers make decisions and go about their other business. "Quaker process" can include discernment, threshing, worship-sharing, clearness, sense of the meeting, and other methodological terms described in this glossary. These constituent aspects have in common a commitment to obedience to the leading of the spirit.

Quarterly Meeting: A regional gathering of members of constituent Monthly Meetings, traditionally on four occasions each year. Some Quarterly Meetings also oversee the operations of institutions.

Queries: A set of questions, based on Friends' practices and testimonies, which are considered by Meetings and individuals as a way of both guiding and examining individual and corporate lives and actions. As such, they are a means of self examination. Queries to be considered regularly are included in *Faith and Practice*; others may be formulated by a committee or Meeting that seeks to clarify for itself an issue it needs to address.

Recording Clerk: The person appointed to take minutes at regular and called meetings for business of a Meeting or other Friends body.

Rightly Ordered: In alignment with the leading of the spirit as discerned by the Meeting or the group empowered with authority in a particular matter. (See Good Order.)

Sense of the Meeting: An expression of the unity of a meeting for worship for business on some issue or concern; the general recognition, articulated by the clerk or some other person, that a given decision is in accordance with the divine will.

Silence/Silent Worship: Expectant, living silence, and not merely the absence of noise. The quietude of Friends meeting for worship — and other periods of observant worship — embodies the special quiet of listeners, the special perception of seekers, the special alertness of those who wait. The silence invites the sharing of messages, which arise from a stirring of the spirit.

Simplicity: One of the traditional Quaker testimonies that is closely associated with integrity, equality, and stewardship. Essentially, to limit the material circumstances of one's life in a way that allows/enables one to follow divine leadings.

Speaking to My/One's Condition: The conviction that a message, whether directly from God or through the words or actions of another, meets one's own deepest needs and purposes.

Standing Aside: An action taken by an individual who has genuine reservations about a particular decision, but who also recognizes that the decision is clearly supported by the weight of the Meeting.

Stewardship: For Friends, stewardship is an element of integrity. Good stewardship directs Friends' investment of time and money in sustainable and renewable resources and in work that supports Quaker values and beliefs.

Testimony: A guiding principle of conduct that bears witness to a spiritual presence in the world and in our lives. Though there is no official list of such testimonies, Friends have traditionally identified peace and nonviolence, equality, simplicity, stewardship, community, and integrity as their practical principles.

Threshing Session: A gathering of Friends to consider in depth a controversial issue but in a way that is free from the necessity of reaching a decision.

Truth: The revealed will of God, as experienced in communion with the Inner Light. Early Quakers called themselves the Religious Society of Friends of the Truth.

Under the Care of: Describes an activity, program, or event for which a Meeting takes responsibility and to which it gives oversight: thus a marriage, a preparative meeting, and a school might all be said to be under the care of a Monthly Meeting. For schools and meetings, see Care Relationship.

Under the Weight of: Giving high priority to an issue arising from a deep feeling of concern. Said of an individual or Meeting that is struggling to reach an appropriate decision about such an item of business.

Unity: The spiritual oneness and harmony whose realization is a primary objective of a meeting for worship or a meeting for business.

Unprogrammed Meeting: A Friends Meeting whose worship is based on quiet waiting for the presence of God revealed through spirit-led vocal ministry and the gathered communion; sometimes called open worship. [cf., Programmed Meeting]

Weighty Friend: An informal term for a Friend who is respected for spiritual depth, wisdom, and long service to the Religious Society of Friends.

Worship Sharing: A modern group practice in which participants share personal and spiritual experiences, thoughts, and feelings, often in response to a prearranged theme or questions, and in a manner that acknowledges the presence of divine guidance.

Yearly Meeting: Those Friends from a geographically extended area who gather in annual session to worship and conduct business together. This term is also used to denote the total membership of the constituent Monthly Meetings of a designated Yearly Meeting.

Appendix A — Resources for Further Study

Friends Council on Education

www.friendscouncil.org
- Governance Consultants
- Governance Tools
- Publications

www.friendscouncil.net
- Friends School Board Clerks
- Friends School Heads
- Business Managers in Friends Schools
- Friends School Trustees

BoardSource, **www.boardsource.org**. Resource for building strong and effective non-profit boards.

Council for American Private Education (CAPE), **www.capenet.org**. National consortium of private schools. Publications on academic and policy matters.

Independent School Management (ISM), **www.isminc.com**. Resource for workshops and materials that can be used for professional development for boards and administrators.

National Association of Independent Schools (NAIS), **www.nais.org**. Source of publications suited professional development, including white papers, case studies, and more. Annual conference.

National Business Officers Association (NBOA), **www.nboa.net**. Information regarding finance, financial aid, and financial sustainability.

The Trustee's Letter and The Head's Letter newsletters, available through Educational Directions, Inc., **www.edu-directions.com**.

Appendix B — Friends Education Position Statements

We hope always to support our students in their development as truly honorable people — informed, engaged, and compassionate people, who come to positions on issues of consequence by active analysis and reflection, informed by a sense of respect for and responsibility toward others, in a spirit defined by neither arrogance nor apathy.

— Lisa Darling, Former Clerk, Friends Council on Education Board of Directors

The Friends Council on Education consists of eighty-five Friends schools, prekindergarten through grade 12, in the United States. As the only national organization of Friends schools, the Friends Council on Education is in a unique position to voice public positions for Friends education.

Academic and Moral Development

For more than 300 years, Friends schools have been recognized for fine academics as well as a whole-child approach to intellectual and moral development. Students are encouraged by word and by example to respect the talents and perspectives of others and include them in a cooperative search for knowledge. The Friends Council on Education affirms that the core purpose of its member schools is to create deliberate learning communities that are centered on Quaker values such as simplicity, peace, justice, stewardship, and integrity.

Access and Affordability

The Friends Council on Education is committed to supporting the diversity of educational choices that make the American educational system unique. Friends schools operate on the founding Quaker principles of equality and diversity, and Friends schools seek to maintain financial aid programs to insure accessibility and affordability.

Diversity and Multiculturalism

Friends schools value and embrace the diversity of cultures and religions in their communities. The curricular approach in Friends education is committed to the rich diversity of multiple perspectives, cultivated through each student's voice engaged in inquiry. Friends schools continually review and change curricula in ways that are responsive to the current world context through studies with artistic and intellectual values that are culturally diverse.

Institutional Independence

The Friends Council on Education affirms that membership in the Friends Council is composed of schools and organizations based on the faith and practice of the Religious Society of Friends (Quakers). The Friends Council on Education is committed to the independence of its member schools, affirming the variety and diversity of these schools and supporting their prerogative to offer an extensive range of curricula and programs, to select quality teachers who meet their criteria, and to create values-based learning communities based on the unique educational missions of their schools.

Peace Education and Nonviolent Conflict Resolution

The Friends Council on Education supports Friends schools in establishing communities that purposefully work with conflict, developing peace education curricula and practices for nonviolent conflict resolution. Friends school curricula and practices promote teaching each subject in a way that enhances student understanding of justice and basic human and civil rights.

Service Learning

The Friends Council on Education affirms that outreach and service learning are embedded in the curricula of Friends schools. Through the civic engagement of service learning, students build and value relationships with others so that an appreciation of the similarities and differences across humanity can be experienced. Students gain an awareness of the world beyond their immediate environment, have exposure to broad societal issues, develop compassion for those struggling under difficult circumstances, cultivate an ability to view problems from a variety of perspectives, and recognize their own capacity to actively make a difference in the world.

World Citizenry

The Friends Council on Education affirms that Friends schools teach values for world citizenry including the love of freedom, religious tolerance, democracy, respect for human dignity, respect for diversity and work to improve the lives of the oppressed. Following Quaker principles, Friends schools seek to incorporate those values into the life and culture of the school, rather than represent them in symbols and rote recitations.